The Stink or the Storm

Michael Brian O'Flaherty

Synesis Press

For Caren,
the love of my life and my best friend.

For Paul and Shannon,
who bring me joy and keep things interesting.

And for our first son,
who is waiting for us in eternity.
His absence on earth makes heaven all the more precious.

When you pass through the waters, I will be with you;
and through the rivers, they shall not overflow you.
When you walk through the fire, you shall not be burned,
nor shall the flame scorch you.

— Isaiah 43:2

Then I will sprinkle clean water on you, and you shall
be clean; I will cleanse you from all your filthiness and
from all your idols.

— Ezekiel 36:25

O Jerusalem, wash your heart from wickedness, that you
may be saved. How long shall your evil thoughts lodge
within you?

— Jeremiah 4:14

Contents

Preface

The Sermon That Planted the Seed

> *Anyone can count the seeds in an apple, but only God knows the number of apples a seed will produce.*
>
> — Author unknown

In the 1980s, I was asked to record sermons at the New Albany church of Christ. Back then, "technology" meant a cassette recorder that clicked like a guillotine when you pressed Record. The whole operation ran on two prayers: that the tape would last, and that I would remember to flip it to Side B before the sermon ran long.

It always did.

On August 27, 1988, a guest speaker named Norman Gendt stepped into the pulpit and preached a sermon titled:

The Stink or the Storm.

He admitted up front that it was a strange title—something a little... smelly.

It stuck anyway.

The sermon was about Noah, the Ark, the church, and baptism.

That sermon planted a seed I didn't fully understand at the time. One that took decades to grow. This book you now hold is what came out of it. Not perfect. Not exhaustive. Not everything I might have said if I had another decade to keep sanding the edges.

But books are not finished so much as released.[1]

At some point, you have to let them go.

Now, a confession.

I've spent years listening to conversations, books, articles, debates, podcasts, and more sermons than I can count. Somewhere along the way, ideas blur. Phrases stick. Insights resurface.

So yes—some of what you'll read here has been "borrowed."

If you recognize something and didn't receive the credit you deserve, that was not intentional. It is the side effect of a long trail of influence and a less-than-perfect memory.

As for the title, I don't know whether Norm heard it somewhere, coined it himself, or had one of those rare flashes of preacherly brilliance. But it stayed with me.

And because of the impact it had on me, this book carries that name in his honor.

Acknowledgments

Those Who Helped It Grow

> *I thank my God upon every remembrance of you...*
>
> Philippians 1:3

There are more people than I can possibly list who shaped me along the way—and a few who probably wondered what took me so long.

If your name isn't here, it's not because you didn't matter. It's because the list is longer than the book.

To my parents, who endured the drumming, the wandering, and my impressive ability to avoid a "normal" career path: thank you. You probably deserved quieter hobbies and safer ambitions.

You got neither.

To my in-laws, who looked at this tall, lanky goof chasing after their beautiful daughter and welcomed me anyway: thank you.

To my family, too many to list, with too much history to capture in a few lines: thank you.

But this acknowledgment would be incomplete if I did not pause to mention my cousins Tim and Janis (Pahasque) Price, and my Aunt Janis Price, whose lives and courage meant more to me than words can carry. Some people leave an imprint you don't fully understand until they're gone. Both Janises did.

To Jeff and Sandy Westerby, along with the entire Westerby and Kirks families: thank you for the early investment. Jeff especially helped plant some of the first seeds and kept me out of more trouble than I'll admit here. Over the years, Jeff and Sandy have faced storms of their own, and they have shown me how to lean hard into faith when life doesn't make sense.

That alone deserves a dedication.

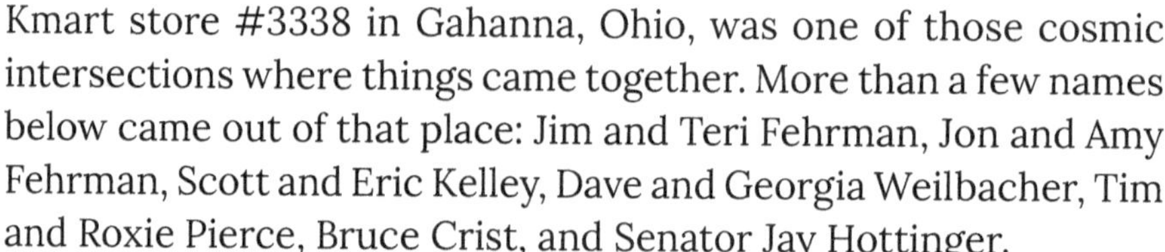

Kmart store #3338 in Gahanna, Ohio, was one of those cosmic intersections where things came together. More than a few names below came out of that place: Jim and Teri Fehrman, Jon and Amy Fehrman, Scott and Eric Kelley, Dave and Georgia Weilbacher, Tim and Roxie Pierce, Bruce Crist, and Senator Jay Hottinger.

On Friday nights, a group of us would end up at Tim's mom's house for Eagles Pizza (world-renowned) and a Bible study. We talked about the church. We wrestled with baptism. We asked questions we didn't always have answers for.

It didn't feel historic at the time.

But it was.

I was baptized on July 2, 1986.

Not long after that, another life-changing moment happened at that same Kmart. This one involved a checkout line.

I found myself going through the register of a cashier named Caren. With a C. That mattered then. It still matters now.

Not long after that, we started dating. Then we got married.

She was my blue light special—and somehow, I'm the one who got the better end of the deal.

We've been happily married ever since.

Over the years, God has put the right people in place at the right time—especially shepherds.

Gail Jacobus, Ben Major, and Norm Stikes showed me what elder-ship is supposed to look like. Not just in title, but in presence, patience, and steadiness. A special shoutout to JoAnn Stikes, who demonstrated strength and faith when life didn't cooperate, especially after Norm passed.

These weren't just servant leaders. They were examples you could follow.

And then there are the elders and church family who put up with me today: John Harris, Dan "Slim Jim" Cuneo, Bobby Spence, and the entire company of saints at the Streetsboro church of Christ. That alone may qualify them for an additional reward.

We've also been blessed by time with other congregations: the New Albany church of Christ, the Ravenna church of Christ, and the Kent church of Christ. The friends and family we found in those places shaped me more than they probably realize, and this book carries some of them with it.

I am thankful for the work being done through Potter Children's Home, Mid-Western Children's Home, Northeastern Ohio Christian Youth Camp, and The MAGI Project. These efforts remind us that the work of the kingdom is not theoretical; it reaches real children, real families, young hearts, and souls in need. We were introduced to The MAGI Project through our dear friend Tessa "the Asset" Hatfield and her wonderful parents, Mark and Jane Hatfield. We are grateful to the Hatfields for sharing Tessa with us while she is in school.

God also surrounded me with encouragers—the kind of people who show up, speak up, and keep you moving when you might otherwise stall out:

Dan Bryne, Nolan and Patty Fuller, Charlie and Lori Houser, Greg and Carolyn Evans, Ryan and Sarah Evans and the Wallick clan, Bellefant, Nick, Stafie, and Bharti (Maa) Christian, Patricia Jordan, Aubrey Konigsberger, Mike Mouser, Professor Robert Sidwell, Jim Tasker, Gabriel Adami, Tony and Dolores McCumbers, Mike and Charlotte Bisson, Doug and Mary Shodd, and Dr. Sam Lewis—who gave me the unforgettable Noahic advice to "fight like the third monkey"—and many more I'm sure I'm forgetting.

And a special shoutout to Brian, Mary, and Aletheia Gould: Aletheia's life was brief, but deeply felt, and Brian and Mary have shown what enduring faith looks like when the storm doesn't pass quickly.

If you've ever had someone believe in you at the right time, you know how much that matters.

Everyone in the church has spiritual parents and grandparents. I am no exception:

Jim and Bobbie Westerby, Wayne and Nancy Walton, Jim and Barbara Mowder, Roy and Wanda Mouser, Karl and Deborah Konigsberger, Paul Golden, and Joe Wallis.

They didn't just teach. They invested.

And finally, the voices.

Those men I've listened to over the years—preachers, teachers, and ministers who helped shape how I think, study, and understand Scripture.

Not a complete list, but a meaningful one:

Jim Mowder, Terry Smith, Bill Craddock, Ralph Price, Brent Harris, David Newberry, Jim McGuiggan, Bill Covan, Phil Grear, Glen Hawkins, Mike Bisson, Greg Evans, Bellefant, Robert Sidwell, Herman McCain, Wayne Walton, Bill Hopkins, Roger Brown, Doug Shodd, David Kenney, Dave Miller, and Jeff Stone, who both baptized me and married us.

And of course, Norm "Stormin' Norman" Gendt.

Still stirring things up, all these years later.

Introduction

Imagine the day an army marched into Kentucky to build a replica of Noah's Ark.[1]

Not a miniature model for kids. Not a Sunday school craft project. A full-scale, lumber-and-sweat reconstruction.

Neighbors shook their heads. Tourists lined up. Reporters scribbled. It looked like a sideshow—too strange to take seriously.

And yet...

Why does the story of an ark still intrigue us thousands of years later?

A boat on dry land feels both ridiculous and, somehow, prophetic.

Which brings us to something just as strange: baptism.

On the surface, it looks like theater: a grown person lowered into water while everyone in the room watches in silence. Ceremonial. Outdated. Maybe even unnecessary.

But that depends on what the water actually means.

Because water, in the story of Scripture, never leaves you where it found you. It carries you somewhere.

The question is where.

The apostle Peter once connected two images most people never think to put together: a Flood and a rescue. Not as decoration. Not as metaphorical wallpaper.

As survival.

And in that story, survival had a place.

This book isn't an argument that the Flood happened. It's an argument that the pattern still does.

That is the tension this book explores.

Because some things only look optional...

until they aren't.

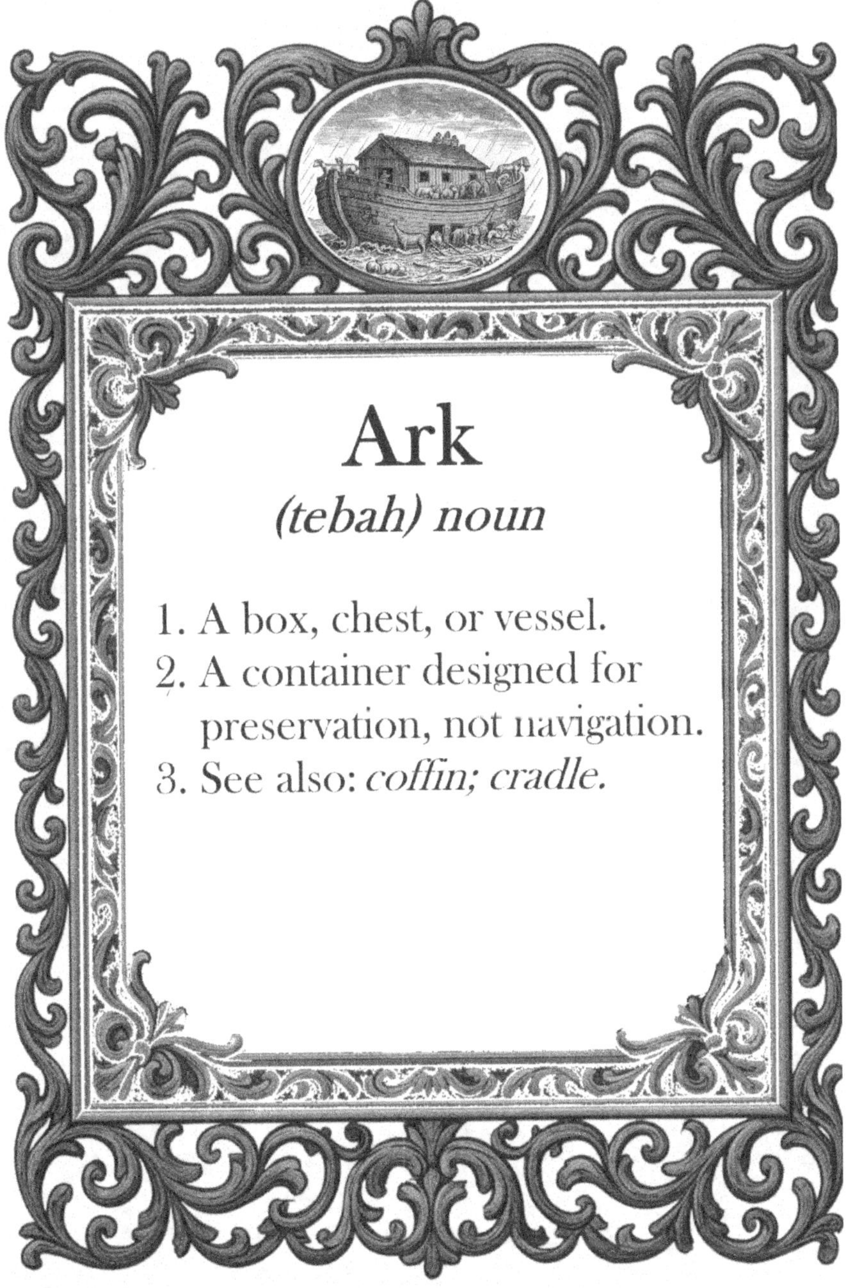

Ark
(tebah) noun

1. A box, chest, or vessel.
2. A container designed for preservation, not navigation.
3. See also: coffin; cradle.

CHAPTER ONE

The Gathering Storm

Before the First Drop Fell

In the beginning God created the heavens and the earth. The earth was without form, and void; and darkness was on the face of the deep. And the Spirit of God was hovering over the face of the waters.

— Genesis 1:1-2

The universe began as a hot mess—literally. God doesn't open His cosmic opera with a cozy garden scene and the gentle strum of harps. It starts with *tohu vavohu*[1]: chaos, darkness, the kind of mess you'd find in your kid's bedroom after a sleepover.

At first, the mess is manageable. A few toys here, a crumpled shirt there. But left alone, it doesn't stay that way. The clutter metastasizes. Socks vanish into the carpet. The smell hardens into something unholy. The room takes on a life of its own.

That's entropy—the slow, stubborn drift from order to chaos.

Think of it as celestial clutter, the universe's built-in tendency toward messiness. It's merciless and unforgiving. Every engineer knows it. So does every parent.

It was against this backdrop that God began His creative work.

> *Then God said, "Let there be light"; and there was light. And God saw the light, that it was good; and God divided the light from the darkness.*
>
> — Genesis 1:3–4

In an instant—*snap!* Light here. Dark there. Land separated from seas. Boundaries established. God organized the chaos by sorting the cosmic junk drawer.

But sorting isn't curing.

Entropy never really goes away. At least, not yet. It lingers in the background, ready to pounce the moment you stop paying attention to it.

It isn't a bug in the system—it *is* the system.

> *Then the Lord God took the man and put him in the garden of Eden to tend and keep it.*
>
> — Genesis 2:15

It was time for the real drama to begin. Adam and Eve stepped onto that stage with a monumental task.

Contrary to popular opinion, paradise came with chores. They were charged with tending the garden, maintaining order, and keeping entropy at bay. It was a perfect system, if only they could have resisted the temptation to distrust the One who gave it to them.

And the serpent?

A polite stagehand, handing them a question with a lie tucked inside it (Genesis 3:1). Suddenly, "enough" didn't feel like enough anymore.

The curtain rose. The orchestra hit a wrong note. Props fell over, and voilà...

Paradise went full improv (Genesis 3:6–7).

Any human society is free to choose either to display great energy or to enjoy sexual freedom; the evidence is that it cannot do both for more than one generation.
— J.D. Unwin, Sex and Culture

In 1934, British anthropologist J.D. Unwin walked into the academic world with a book so dense and uncompromising that most people ignored it. *Sex and Culture*[2] was the kind of title you expect to find gathering dust on a library shelf.

But his thesis was dynamite. Buried beneath those charts and footnotes was a story about why civilizations rise, shine, and fall.

Unwin's conclusion was as simple as it was unsettling: the fate of a society depends on what it does with sex.

Not politics.
Not economics.
Not military genius.

Sex.

When cultures disciplined sexual desire through chastity and family, they built institutions, invented mathematics, launched empires.

Unwin spent years peering into the skeleton closets of eighty cultures. Sumerians. Romans. Tribes without names. He came back with a shocking verdict nobody wanted to hear: sex rules destiny.

When societies loosened those rules, cultural energy drained away.

Every. Single. Time.
No exceptions.

It almost sounds superstitious. Give up your impulses, and in return you get art, science, and architecture.

Unwin wasn't religious about it. He didn't frame his discovery in a moral sermon. This was anthropology, plain and simple.

Contain sexual energy, and civilization shoots upward like a rocket. Let that energy leak out, and society fizzles like a punctured tire.

You can see why his work never became a bestseller. Who wants to hear that personal freedom is the seed of destruction? This isn't a sermon the world is lining up to hear. But the ruins of Rome, the fall of Babylon, the fading of Greece—they all hum the same tune.

Ironically, it isn't about sex at all. It's about *energy*. Sex just happens to be the most powerful reservoir of it.

A culture can spend its energy on discipline and creation, or it can spend it on pleasure and comfort. But not both. Sooner or later, the bill comes due.

We are free to choose our pleasures, but discipline determines destiny.

Then the Lord saw that the wickedness of man was great in the earth, and that every intent of the thoughts of his heart was only evil continually.
— Genesis 6:5

What Unwin saw through data, the Bible declared long ago.

Within ten generations after Eden, people stopped pushing back on entropy (Genesis 5). Families crumbled. Power twisted sex into a commodity. Men chose women the way shoppers pick fruit: pretty, disposable, replaceable (Genesis 6:2).

These unions produced the Nephilim, the "fallen ones"—generations bred on chaos (Genesis 6:4).

Civilization began to crack. The primordial mess returned.

And God said to Noah, "The end of all flesh has come before Me, for the earth is filled with violence through them; and behold, I will destroy them with the earth.
— Genesis 6:13

If your computer has ever frozen mid-sentence while you were writing something important, you'll recognize the feeling. That helpless moment when the system locks up and nothing responds.

The Creator who sculpted galaxies watched His masterpiece rot from the inside out. Every heartbeat that once pulsed with purpose turned septic. Violence became entertainment. Beauty became bait. Love became appetite.

The system wasn't glitching. It was dying.

God wasn't shocked—omniscience doesn't do surprise. But He was grieved. Deep, aching pain filled His heart (Genesis 6:6). Not rage. Pain. The kind that comes when you've poured everything into something beautiful just to watch it rot beyond repair.

So God made the decision only a Creator can make. He wouldn't unmake what He loved, but He would reset it (Genesis 6:7).

A hard restart for a system that refused to heal itself.

> But as the days of Noah were, so also will the coming of the Son of Man be.
>
> — Matthew 24:37

Sound familiar?

History doesn't repeat itself, but it often rhymes. The world before Noah was prosperous, self-assured, and hollow. The storm didn't arrive without warning. It arrived without listeners (Matthew 24:38–39).

The same pattern buzzes beneath our headlines. Pleasure without purpose. Freedom without restraint. These aren't trends—they're red flags.

Which brings us back to the messy bedroom.

A parent can either inject energy to restore order or step back and let chaos take over. Order isn't natural. Chaos is. Stop paddling upstream, and the current decides the direction for you.

If you want stability, you must fight for it.

Every. Single. Time.
No exceptions.

CHAPTER TWO

The Gopherwood Box

God Wasn't Vague on Purpose

> *We place absolute confidence in the Titanic. We believe that the boat is unsinkable.*[1]
>
> — Philip A. S. Franklin, VP of White Star Line

On April 14, 1912, just before midnight, Dr. Washington Dodge felt the shudder of history.[2]

A respected banker and politician from San Francisco, he was sailing home aboard the RMS *Titanic*, the greatest ship ever built. Powered by massive engines, this steel colossus was the "unsinkable" triumph of human ingenuity.

But one iceberg later, that confidence was gone.

Moments after the collision, Dodge stepped into the corridor, confused but calm. An officer passing by assured him it was nothing more than a minor issue. No danger. No reason to wake his family.

Hours later, Dodge stood on the freezing deck of a dying ship. He placed his wife and son into a lifeboat. Later, amid the chaos, he was pushed into another lifeboat, one of only a handful of men from first class to survive. At 2:20 a.m., he watched as the *Titanic* snapped in half and slipped beneath the black waters of the Atlantic. The lights vanished. The screams faded. The promise of the "unsinkable" became a tomb. That lie cost fifteen hundred people their lives.

He lived. But he didn't survive.

For the rest of his life, Washington Dodge was haunted by that night. He returned to San Francisco wealthy, respected, outwardly thriving but inwardly hollow. Seven years later, he took his own life. Perhaps the man who survived humanity's proudest vessel carried the quiet torment of having lived when so many others did not.

Confidence is fragile. Pride is fatal (Proverbs 16:18). And the wrong vessel will break you.

Because when judgment comes, the question is never whether the storm is real. It's whether the vessel is trustworthy.

> *She is a new wonder of the world ... a floating city of incomparable splendor.*[3]
>
> — The Shipbuilder Magazine, 1911

At 882 feet, the *Titanic* was the largest moving object on Earth. To walk her decks was to step into an age that believed progress could look God in the eye and not blink. Sleek. Opulent. Untouchable. A floating monument to human hubris.

To board her was to leave the world behind. Oak-paneled dining rooms. A grand staircase crowned by glass. Chandeliers glittering above velvet lounges. It even featured a gymnasium with mechanical horses and a Turkish bath. Passengers dined on porcelain and slept beneath carved mahogany ceilings.

The *Titanic* was more than a ship. It was proof, so they thought, of human mastery over nature.

It's tempting to picture the Ark as something grand, something elegant. Many of us do. Blame children's books and cartoons, with smiling giraffes poking their heads out of portholes.

But this was no cruise ship.

At 450 feet, roughly half the length of the *Titanic*, it held no marble columns, no orchestra, no champagne. The Ark was a wooden box: ugly, massive, stubborn. Built for one purpose only: survival.

Here's the paradox. The *Titanic* was built by professionals. The Ark was built by amateurs. One lies at the bottom of the ocean. The other saved the world.

Genius is not a requirement for salvation (1 Corinthians 1:27). Obedience is.

The Ark wasn't designed to impress; it was designed to endure.[4]

But Noah found grace in the eyes of the Lord... And God said to Noah, "The end of all flesh has come before Me, for the earth is filled with violence through them; and behold, I will destroy them with the earth."
— Genesis 6:8,13

The Ark reminds us that even when God judges, He is already preparing rescue. Judgment is never His final word. Mercy is. Even before the first cloud gathered, there was a promise.

When humanity shattered Eden's order, God did not curse and walk away. He whispered a counterplan: the seed of the woman would one day crush the serpent's head (Genesis 3:15). It was cryptic then, but that promise pulsed beneath every page that followed.

God's aim was never annihilation; it was preservation. A vessel. A remnant. A path through the storm.

Mercy doesn't abandon. It prepares.

> By faith Noah, being divinely warned of things not yet seen, moved with godly fear, prepared an ark for the saving of his household, by which he condemned the world and became heir of the righteousness which is according to faith.
>
> — Hebrews 11:7

What kind of person builds something no one else believes is necessary?

The hardest part of Noah's obedience wasn't the labor. It was the laughter.

For 120 years, he was the local eccentric (Genesis 6:3). The conspiracy theorist. The fool with a hammer and a sermon no one asked for (2 Peter 2:5).

Grace put Noah to work. God commanded him to construct a vessel large enough to carry the future. He traded ease for splinters, comfort for calluses. Every plank, every nail, every drop of pitch was a sermon to skeptics who passed by.

It's easy to laugh at a boat when the sky is blue. But the first drop of rain silenced the laughter.

Noah chose ridicule for a century so he could choose survival for eternity. This was obedience in motion: faith taking the physical shape of a rescue.

Entropy had swallowed the world. But inside that wooden box, the righteous survived.

Judgment drowns. Mercy floats.

Make yourself an ark of gopherwood; make rooms in the ark, and cover it inside and outside with pitch. And this is how you shall make it: The length of the ark shall be three hundred cubits, its width fifty cubits, and its height thirty cubits.

— Genesis 6:14–15

When the narrative turns to the Ark's design, the tone shifts. The thunder of judgment gives way to quiet precision.

God measures. God specifies. God details. Nothing is arbitrary. Salvation isn't improvised. It has structure and boundaries. No guesswork.

Grace, it turns out, is engineered. It's not a feeling. It's *architecture*.

Redemption doesn't erase chaos; it constructs shelter.

And that's what mercy does: it builds boundaries strong enough to hold grace.

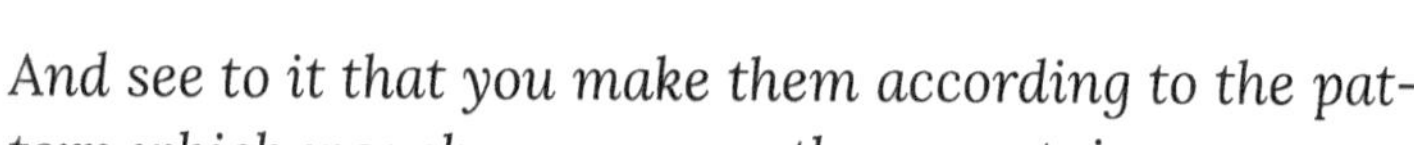

And see to it that you make them according to the pattern which was shown you on the mountain.
— Exodus 25:40

There's a divine irony here. The God who spoke the universe into existence chose to involve human hands in saving it. If the Ark was God's design, obedience was found in Noah's hammer.

A blueprint means nothing without a builder willing to trust it. Noah built what looked foolish because God said it mattered. Divine mercy, though sovereign in origin, always partners with human response. God provides the pattern; faith brings it to life.

What if Noah had modified the design? The warning in Exodus applies here: God's patterns aren't suggestions. They are structures designed to save. This isn't micromanagement—it's rescue.

Noah couldn't calm the storm, but he could follow the pattern.

That's the history of redemption in a single thought: Eden had gardeners. The Ark had a craftsman. Grace always invites partnership.

And faith always looks like someone holding a hammer (James 2:17).

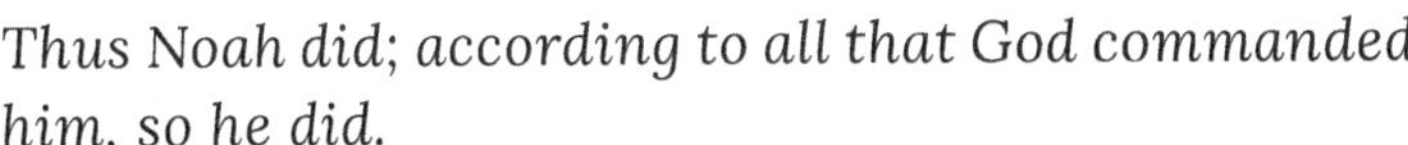

Thus Noah did; according to all that God commanded him, so he did.

> — Genesis 6:22

Noah becomes the archetype of the believer. He couldn't see the full picture, but he trusted the divine Architect. He couldn't predict the storm, but he could build the shelter.

Two vessels. Two promises. One promised *comfort*. The other promised *salvation*. One sought to conquer the sea and vanished beneath it. The other rose on the very waters meant to destroy it.

Luxury can numb you. Comfort can lie. But obedience endures.

We live in an age that mocks divine structure. We've grown suspicious of God's patterns—church, family, community—and rebrand that suspicion as progress. We want an ark, but only if the world approves the design.

The world will never authorize its own judgment. If you wait for permission to obey, you will drown in the waiting room.

To the world, obedience looks like madness. But when the sky turns black, the mockery stops.

Suddenly, the fool with the hammer is the only one prepared for the rain.

It's better to be in an ark that looks strange than on a ship that looks certain (Matthew 7:24–27).

Salvation is a gift. Sanctuary is built: timber by timber, choice by choice. We build what God commands, not what the world admires.

Noah wasn't asked to design the Ark or calm the storm. He was asked to follow the pattern and finish the job.

And when judgment came, the pattern held.

Chapter Three

The Stink

It's Supposed to Smell Like This

> And of every living thing of all flesh you shall bring two of every sort into the ark, to keep them alive with you; they shall be male and female.
>
> — Genesis 6:19

Spend a day on a farm and you learn quickly that time is not measured by clocks, but by appetites. Before the sun rises, life is already awake—hooves shifting, feathers ruffling, low grunts of hunger echoing from dark stalls. Minutes mean nothing. Stomachs rule everything.

What surprises most people isn't the labor, but its relentlessness. Animals don't rest for holidays or sentiment. They eat when they eat. They soil what you just cleaned. And if you are responsible for them, your life bends around that unyielding rhythm.

Feeding.
Watering.

Cleaning.
Mending.

It's not a checklist so much as a pulse. Sleep can wait. A dirty stall can't.

Then there's the smell.

Every farm has one, and every farmer will tell you it never truly leaves. It's more than manure, though that's its foundation. It's life pressed too close together: the sharp tang of urine, the must of hay, the sourness of fermentation, the mineral scent of trampled soil.

It clings to your clothes, your hands, your boots—even your soul.

There's truth in that smell: life, unfiltered, isn't sterile.

The work is an endless grind. You repair one fence and another fails. You scrub a trough and within the hour it's fouled again. You patch, scrape, scrub, and sweep, only to wake to the same glorious mess. The animals, for all their innocence, undo your order as quickly as you impose it.

Order is temporary; disorder is patient. This is entropy at work.

Yet amid the fatigue and rancid odor, something sacred remains. This is how living things are kept alive. Not by a single effort, but by continual tending.

It isn't pretty. It isn't pure. But it's *alive*.

So He destroyed all living things which were on the
face of the ground: both man and cattle, creeping thing

and bird of the air. They were destroyed from the earth. Only Noah and those who were with him in the ark remained alive. And the waters prevailed on the earth one hundred and fifty days.

— Genesis 7:23–24

Now imagine being inside the Ark for an entire year.

A floating ecosystem. No plumbing. No escape. Thousands of animals confined to a wooden stink box. Every sound—a bleat, a bray, a hiss, a flutter—became the soundtrack of survival. The air was thick with the steam of panicked breath.

Somewhere between the creaking timbers and the disaster raging outside, life was negotiating an uneasy truce with confinement.

Noah's task wasn't heroic; it was managerial. He was part zookeeper, part janitor, part priest.

Every creature demanded attention on its own schedule. Predators paced in the dark. Birds rustled restlessly. Livestock chewed slowly, oblivious to the world drowning outside. There were no quiet hours—only the shifting timbre of chaos. A constant reminder that creation doesn't pause for catastrophe.

Noah learned what every farmer already knows: faith isn't about control; it's about maintenance. It wasn't only endurance; it was stewardship. The hands that built the Ark now scraped floors, filled troughs, soothed panic, and cleaned filth. Neglect any one of those tasks, and life inside the Ark would fail.

The Ark didn't hum with precision or ease.

It sweated.
It groaned.

And it stank.

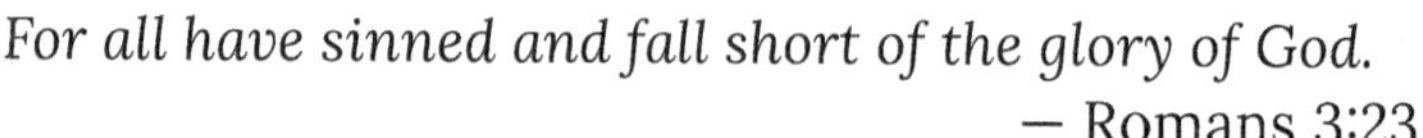

For all have sinned and fall short of the glory of God.
— Romans 3:23

Many people imagine the church as a luxury yacht, a romanticized vessel of perfect harmony. But step aboard, and you quickly realize it's full of stinkers who smell a lot more like the Ark than heaven.

There is friction. Grumbling. People tripping over their own halos.

Holiness, as it turns out, doesn't erase odor; it teaches us how to live with it (Colossians 3:13).

We have this treasure in earthen vessels, that the excellence of the power may be of God and not of us.
— 2 Corinthians 4:7

Paul names our reality without the romance. An "earthen vessel" is a clay pot. Cheap. Fragile. Common. And if you use a clay pot long enough, it cracks.

We are, quite literally, crackpots.

This isn't a defect in God's design. It's the point. If the vessel were gold and the people inside perfect, we would worship the vessel itself.

Cracked clay cannot hold glory. It leaks it.

The value isn't in the pot. It's in the treasure sealed inside.

There's an old saying: "*If you find the perfect church, don't join it because you'll ruin it.*"

That line isn't cynical; it's honest. God didn't choose us for our fragrance, but for purpose. He filled the church with sinners in various stages of renovation, all learning to live with cracks of their own (1 Timothy 1:15).

The church, like the Ark, isn't holy because of who's in it.

It's holy because of Who holds it together.

For we are to God the fragrance of Christ among those who are being saved and among those who are perishing.
— 2 Corinthians 2:15–16

There's irony in the stink.

Noah and his family had to shovel dung out of the Ark. That responsibility didn't end with the Flood.

We shovel pride. We shovel bitterness. We shovel self-interest. That work never ends. In that labor, grace becomes tangible. Without it, rot sets in.

To the world, the church smells offensive. It reeks of restriction and hypocrisy. Outsiders see the mess and assume decay. They confuse the packaging with the contents.

The *Titanic* smelled of lavender, brandy, and fresh paint, yet it was a coffin. It carried the aroma of death disguised as luxury.

The Ark smelled of manure, sweat, and wet fur, yet it was a cradle. It carried the aroma of life disguised as labor.

You shall make a window for the ark, and you shall finish it to a cubit from above.

— Genesis 6:16

There is one architectural detail worth lingering over.

God commanded Noah to build a window—but to finish it from above. That detail matters. It was mercy by design.

Noah couldn't look out. He couldn't watch bodies drift past. He couldn't fixate on the violence of the storm or the illusion of the horizon. While knee-deep in filth, overwhelmed by noise, smell, and exhaustion, his only light came from above.

Direction didn't come from surveying the chaos; it came from receiving light.

We were never designed to stare endlessly at the mess. We were designed to look upward, toward the Captain who holds the vessel together (Colossians 3:2).

But that window served another purpose. With the door sealed shut by God, the Ark had only one opening left: above (Genesis 7:16). Filth accumulated daily, and there was no back door to sweep it through. The only way out was up.

The Ark didn't run on denial. The mess had to be lifted deliberately toward the light.

The work was repetitive. Humbling. Unavoidable.

The shovel isn't for *others* first. It's for us. We shovel pride before it hardens. We remove bitterness before it ferments. We pitch self-interest and old sins that quietly pile up if left unattended (Hebrews 12:1).

No one outgrows this work. No one is exempt.

Life inside the Ark was shared labor. One family. Many stalls. One window. No one pretended the stink wasn't there. No one waited for perfection before picking up a shovel. Survival depended on dirty hands, not appearance (Galatians 6:2).

If you fixate *only* on the shovel, you grow bitter. If you fixate *only* on the window, you grow passive.

But when you work with your hands and lift your eyes, you endure.

Don't come looking for a spotless vessel. Come ready to shovel.

This stink—this struggle, this stubborn grace—isn't evidence of failure. It's the aroma of life being preserved.

The Ark didn't save because it was impressive.

It saved because God sealed it, sustained it, and taught the people inside to tend what He preserved.

Chapter Four

The Storm

When the Door Closed

> *In the six hundredth year of Noah's life, in the second month, the seventeenth day of the month, on that day all the fountains of the great deep were broken up, and the windows of heaven were opened. And the rain was on the earth forty days and forty nights.*
> — Genesis 7:11–12

Every so often, lightning strikes the ground, and a quiet miracle begins disguised as catastrophe.

Consider the lodgepole pine, a tree found across the forests of Yellowstone and the Sierra Nevada. For years, ecologists were baffled by a strange mystery. Decades of "conservation" left entire forests weak, brittle, and geriatric. Suppress every fire, and the forest doesn't thrive. The canopy thickens until sunlight can no longer reach the forest floor. The soil, choked by layers of dead needles, loses its nutrients and suffocates.[1]

The very abundance that built the forest eventually kills it, unless something intervenes.

That seems cruel until you look at the biology of the tree itself. Lodgepole cones are sealed by rock-hard resin and hang dormant for years. It takes fire to melt the resin, snap the cone open, and release the seeds.

When the fire finally comes, it feels apocalyptic. Old giants fall. Smoke fills the air. From a distance, it looks like death has won.

But then the ash settles.

The soil, now cleared of the dead undergrowth, breathes again. Sunlight reaches the ground. The seeds that could never sprout in the shadows finally take root. Within a season, the forest hums with green again—fresher, freer, younger.

This is what renewal looks like.

Fire isn't the enemy; stagnation is. That slow slide into entropy masquerading as peace.

The blaze isn't only wrath. It's mercy wearing war paint.

God, it seems, isn't afraid to burn down what's broken to save what's essential (John 15:2).

If He withholds the waters, they dry up; if He sends them out, they overwhelm the earth.

— Job 12:15

In the wilderness of Judea, a "river" is often nothing more than a scar in the earth. A dry channel. A *wadi* that looks like it hasn't seen water since the Bronze Age.

It looks dead. It feels dead. You can walk its sandy floor for hours beneath a blazing sun, surrounded by bleached stones, convinced the land has been asleep for centuries.

But Bedouin shepherds know better.

They refuse to camp on the wadi floor, even when the sky is clear and the ground is dry. They understand that the wadi is not empty. It's a place where the earth remembers.

The danger isn't in the rain you *can* see. It's the storm happening miles away that you *can't*. Long before the first drop falls, you hear it: a low, distant rumble, like a heavy stone being dragged across the sky.

Flash floods don't build slowly. They come as a wall of mud and water with the force of a tidal wave. Nobody outruns it. Not the shepherd. Not the wanderer with good cardio. A man standing in ankle-deep dust can be swept away before he understands what is happening.

The ancient world understood this. They knew how the earth sleeps, how it remembers, and how, in the blink of an eye, it wakes.

Judgment doesn't ask if you're ready. It just kicks the door in (1 Thessalonians 5:3).

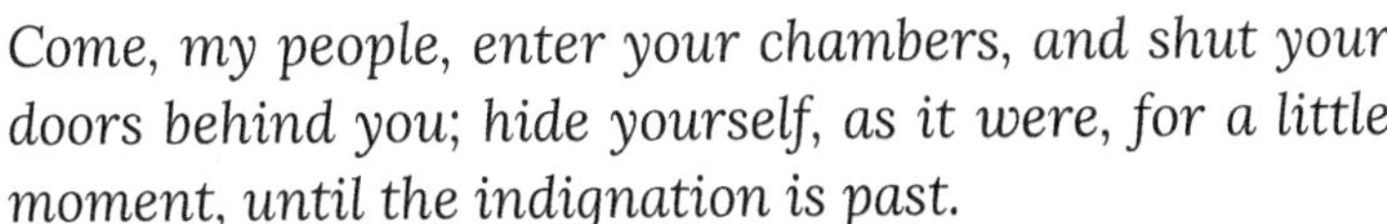

Come, my people, enter your chambers, and shut your doors behind you; hide yourself, as it were, for a little moment, until the indignation is past.
— Isaiah 26:20

When we imagine the Flood, we tend to picture a rainstorm: gray skies and wet umbrellas.

But the text describes something far more violent. It wasn't just the rain from above; it was the upheaval from below. The fountains of the deep were broken open. The earth stopped holding itself together. Everything Noah's neighbors trusted as solid liquefied.

But judgment didn't begin with the rain. It began with the sound of a door closing.

Genesis contains a chilling sentence: "And the Lord shut him in" (Genesis 7:16).

One door. Shut from the outside. Once closed, the world was gone.

Eight souls sat in the darkness, listening to the roar of a world being unmade—and the screams of the lost.

For there is hope for a tree, if it is cut down, that it will sprout again, and that its tender shoots will not cease.
— Job 14:7

We wonder why the people of Noah's day were caught off guard. Jesus gives us the answer. They ate. They drank. They married (Matthew 24:38). Life felt ordinary—right up until it *wasn't*.

They weren't necessarily wicked. They were distracted, lulled by routine, convinced that tomorrow would look like today.

We are no different. Normalcy is a powerful drug. It persuades us that the party will never end.

The Flood wasn't malice. It was triage: the clearing of what was dead so that what remained could breathe again.

Look also at ships: although they are so large and are driven by fierce winds, they are turned by a very small rudder wherever the pilot desires.

— James 3:4

Noah wasn't floating—he was *adrift*.

The Ark lacked everything we associate with control: no rudder, no oars, no wheel. If you saw it today, you wouldn't call it a ship. You'd call it a wooden box, something built to survive, not chart a course.

Noah couldn't aim for safety or outrun destruction. He couldn't dodge debris or adjust his heading. The Ark moved where the water carried it.

Yet the Ark didn't drift aimlessly. Noah wasn't navigating a crisis. He was being carried through one.

This goes against our instincts. We want dashboards and levers, plans and contingencies. When things fall apart, we reach for control, convinced that steering harder will save us.

The opposite is true. The Ark was safe precisely because Noah *couldn't* control it (Proverbs 16:9).

Sometimes it's safest inside a boat you can't steer, carried by Someone who *can*.

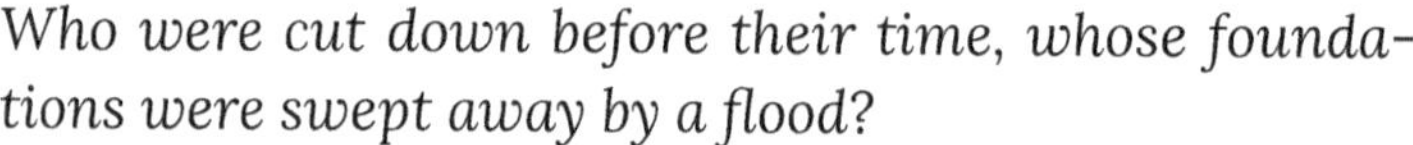

Who were cut down before their time, whose founda-
tions were swept away by a flood?

— Job 22:16

What did Noah feel when the door closed?

Relief, perhaps. Grief, certainly.

We like to think we could handle that horrifying realization—that everyone we love is on the wrong side of the door. We probably couldn't. I doubt Noah could, either.

But once the door shut, there was nothing more to build and nothing more to explain. Only pitch. And promise.

Which brings us back to the forest.

The Ark was the ultimate pinecone: a lifeboat sealed with pitch, holding the very seeds of humanity waiting to be freed. Like seeds, they had no control over where they would be planted. All they could do was wait.

Eventually, the storm passed. The waters receded. The world emerged fresher, freer, younger. Humanity was given another chance to take root (Genesis 9:1).

The door didn't just open—it exhaled.

And life began again.

CHAPTER FIVE

The War Bow

Why Judgment Isn't the End of the Story

> *Then God remembered Noah, and every living thing, and all the animals that were with him in the ark. And God made a wind to pass over the earth, and the waters subsided.*
>
> — Genesis 8:1

Astronauts don't talk much about fear. They talk about systems, protocols, mission objectives. They're engineers, pilots, checklist people.

They train for everything: fire, radiation, systems failure, panic. They trust the mathematics of the unseen. To them, feelings get in the way of clean execution.

But there's one thing no simulator prepares them for: the window.

The first time an astronaut looks back at Earth, something unexpected happens. They stop thinking like operators and start thinking like observers. The planet no longer looks like a map of competing interests and borders. It looks like a shimmering organism, suspended in a sea of black.

Beautiful.
And terrifying.

Some say it feels euphoric. Others say it hurts—an ache at seeing a world so serene and delicate. From space, the planet doesn't look powerful. It looks exposed. Temporary. Vulnerable. With no backup.

Psychologists call this the *Overview Effect*.[1]

Part awe, part terror. A maternal instinct to protect what is fragile. Once you see it, you can't pretend the world is disposable anymore.

Astronauts go up as specialists. They come down as witnesses.

And oddly enough, it's the perfect way to understand Noah.

He was the first to experience the Overview Effect without ever entering orbit. He didn't need a rocket or a spacesuit. He just needed a boat—and a front-row seat to the end of the world.

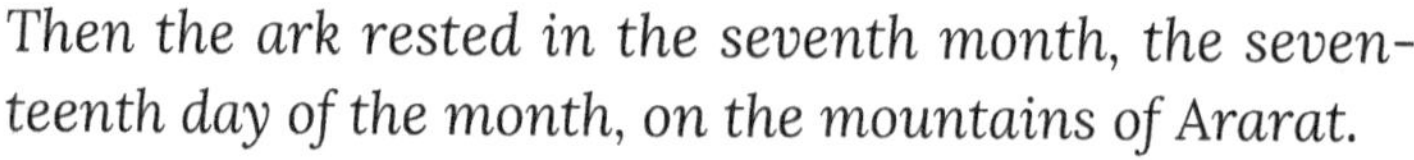

> *Then the ark rested in the seventh month, the seventeenth day of the month, on the mountains of Ararat.*
> — Genesis 8:4

When the Ark finally rested and the door opened, Noah didn't step back into normal life. There was no normal left. He stepped out into a silent planet, untouched by memory.

He had spent a year in a void, rocking between judgment and mercy, cut off from sky and soil, listening to rain rewrite history.

But the old world?

Gone.
Not damaged, not altered.
Gone.

Noah wasn't coming home; he was landing on a new world.

The water had stripped away everything familiar. No cities. No songs. No graves to visit.

The smell was different. The air felt unused. The hum of civilization had vanished, replaced by a quiet so deep it made him aware of his own bones.

It was as if someone had pulled the plug on the entire human project.

If astronauts get the Overview Effect by drifting above the world, Noah experienced it by surviving beneath it. He saw Earth's fragility not because he left it, but because he watched it drown.

Different altitude. Same revelation.

I set My rainbow in the cloud, and it shall be for the sign of the covenant between Me and the earth.
— Genesis 9:13

Then God does something unexpected.

Noah builds an altar (Genesis 8:20). God responds with a rainbow.

We tend to see the rainbow as celestial artistry—a soft ending to a hard story. God's way of saying, "Sorry about the Flood… here's something colorful." A greeting card from heaven after the storm retreats.

Except that's not what the text says.

The ancient Hebrew suggests something far more warlike. The word isn't about color at all. The Hebrew word is *qesheth*—the same word used throughout the Old Testament for a "battle bow."[2]

This isn't decoration or art.

It's disarmament.

In the ancient Near East, peace wasn't declared only with speeches or treaties. It was declared with posture. The warrior didn't just lower his weapon. He turned it away.

A bow bent for battle aims the arrow at the enemy. But the rainbow is bent backward. The string faces the earth. The arrow points toward the heavens. It's a weapon hung in the sky, aimed not at the survivors, but at the Archer Himself.

A public act of restraint.

Then Genesis adds a strange detail. God says, "I will look on it to remember the everlasting covenant."

Which raises questions.

Is God forgetful? Does omniscience need a cosmic sticky note?

No.

In Scripture, remembering isn't about *memory*. It's about *action*.

A covenant "sign" functions as a legal trigger. When Scripture says God remembers, it doesn't mean He recalls something He forgot. It means He *acts* (Exodus 2:24).

The rainbow isn't for us. We're not the target audience.

God is.

God hung the bow in the clouds not just to comfort Noah, but to bind His own hand. Every time the clouds gather, He looks at the weapon turned away from the earth and restrains Himself (Isaiah 54:9).

The world doesn't endure because humans behave. It endures because God remembers.

That's the difference between sentiment and security.

The battle was over. The judgment finished.

But the long work of rebuilding had only just begun.

The imagination of man's heart is evil from his youth.
                                              — Genesis 8:21

Then, almost immediately, it all falls apart.

There's a postscript most Sunday School teachers skip. It's the moment the hero fails.

Noah, the "righteous man," face-plants three verses into the new world. The farmer cultivates a vineyard, goes on a bender, and passes out in all his righteous glory. His son Ham walks in, sees the mess, and mocks him (Genesis 9:20–22).

And just like that, the family that had been saved from the water begins drowning in dysfunction.

What happened?

Here's the uncomfortable truth about the first Ark: it kept them alive, but it couldn't make them new. The Flood washed the earth. It didn't wash the man.

Eight passengers. One disease. All carrying the same sickness that killed the old world.

Sin didn't drown. It rode shotgun (Proverbs 20:9).

Thus I establish My covenant with you: Never again shall all flesh be cut off by the waters of the flood; never again shall there be a flood to destroy the earth.
                                        — Genesis 9:11

The storm was over, the weapon set aside. The first Ark had done its work. Noah survived; the world continued.

But continuation isn't redemption. Entropy was backstage, waiting for its cue.

The earth was spared, not healed. Judgment was restrained, not resolved.

The shadow had served its purpose. It showed the shape of salvation, but it didn't complete it.

The world still needed saving. It needed the real thing.

It needed the True Ark.

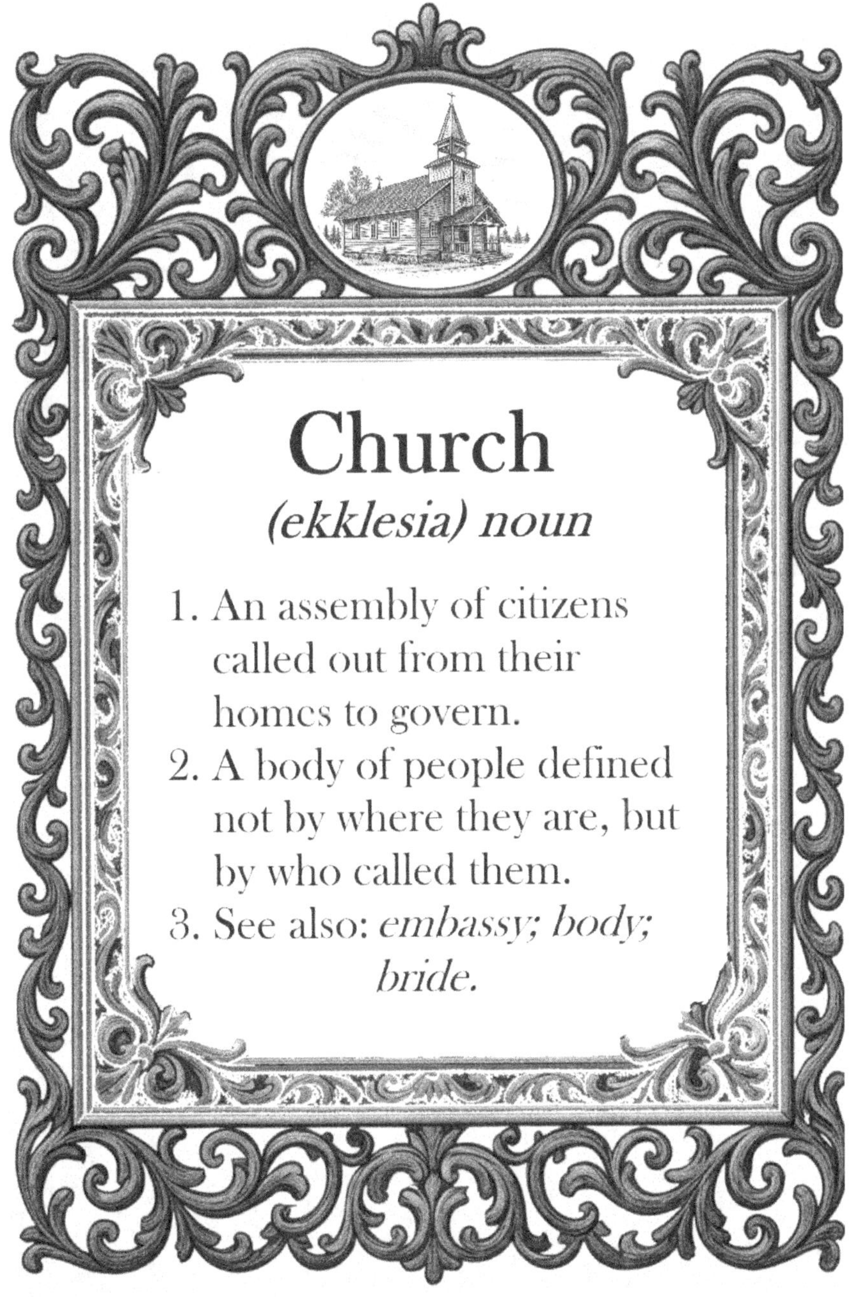

Church

(ekklesia) noun

1. An assembly of citizens called out from their homes to govern.
2. A body of people defined not by where they are, but by who called them.
3. See also: *embassy; body; bride.*

CHAPTER SIX

The Gyroscope

What Keeps You from Tipping Over

> *Your word is a lamp to my feet and a light to my path.*
> — Psalm 119:105

God never asked us to locate truth by instinct, consensus, or sincerity (Jeremiah 17:9).

If the Ark of today is real, it must be identifiable.

Not whether it exists, but how to find it.

In the spring of 2019, pilots flying over the United States found themselves in an unnerving situation. Their instruments—those quiet, trustworthy companions that told them where they were and where they were going—suddenly began to lie.[1]

The GPS signals they depended on were scrambled by a military jamming test, and within minutes, flight paths began to unravel.

Planes drifted off course.
Radios crackled.
Pilots circled, struggling to reorient.

A few came dangerously close to restricted airspace—which, in case you're wondering, isn't the kind of surprise the Pentagon finds amusing.

These weren't amateurs. They weren't careless. They were professionals: trained, disciplined, methodical. The kind of people who can nail a landing in a nasty crosswind and still make it home for brunch.

The problem wasn't their skill.

The system they trusted had stopped telling the truth.

The grass withers, the flower fades, But the word of our God stands forever.

— Isaiah 40:8

When satellites go dark, pilots don't start guessing. They don't innovate or trust their instincts. They go old school: paper charts, compass headings, fixed bearings—real lines, real north.

Because when the system starts lying, you don't need innovation.

You need truth.

A gyroscope doesn't depend on the signal. It doesn't ask the world where north is. It holds orientation when the instruments around it begin to lie.

That's what Scripture does.

It does not flatter our instincts. It does not drift with consensus. It does not update itself to match the age. It tells us which way is up when the whole cockpit is spinning.

To call it "just a book" is to undersell it. The Bible reveals the very mind of God. Written by more than forty authors across sixteen centuries, on three continents, and in multiple languages, it still speaks with one voice.

It tells us what God loves, what He hates, what He rescues, and what He judges. It tells us where mercy is found—and where it *isn't*.

That's the part most of us want to negotiate.

But a fixed bearing doesn't apologize for being narrow. A runway is narrow. A doorway is narrow. The Ark was narrow.

Let's be honest: most people are perfectly comfortable owning a copy of that "dusty old book" but secretly hope there's nothing too binding inside.

Yet the Bible doesn't just contain truth; it claims to be *absolute* truth, breathed out by God Himself (2 Timothy 3:16). It's living, powerful, and sharper than any two-edged sword (Hebrews 4:12).

To some, that sounds presumptuous.

But to those who have tested it, who have staked their lives on its promises, Scripture is less a collection of pages and more an anchor dropped into eternity.

Every generation thinks it's outsmarted this thing. Ours is no exception.

Kings have burned it.
Scholars have dismissed it.
Multitudes have ignored it.

Philosophers, scientists, and reformers insisted that humanity had matured beyond the need for this ancient text. And yet, the Bible remains in the background of civilization, still quoted at weddings and funerals, still showing up in political speeches by people who may or may not have actually read it.

It outlasts empires and transcends culture. Its words have steadied slaves and emperors alike, guided the hands of law-givers and poets, and comforted those who had nothing left to hold onto.

The instruments that guide us today—technology, opinion, even our own feelings—are unreliable.

The Bible does not drift.

It does not change.

It does not need updates.

> *For assuredly, I say to you, till heaven and earth pass away, one jot or one tittle will by no means pass from the law till all is fulfilled.*
>
> — Matthew 5:18

Jesus Himself spoke of Scripture this way: not as a flexible guide, but as something so fixed that even the smallest stroke couldn't fail. Its authority doesn't rest on popularity, progress, or votes; it rests on the character of the One who spoke it.

That's why the Bible isn't just a reference manual for the religious. It is the calibration for our conscience, the standard by which every other instrument is judged. It tells us who God is, who we are, and what "good" truly means.

And yet, orientation only works when we follow it.

You can ignore it, sure. You can put it back on the shelf and pretend you know the way. But the Bible's words aren't diminished by our neglect. Only our direction is.

When we trust the instruments of our own making, we inevitably find ourselves lost, circling the sky without a bearing, wondering how far we've drifted from home.

Ignoring true north doesn't make life more authentic. It makes it impossible to find your way back.

Scripture doesn't adjust itself to our motion. It corrects it.

The world never lost the signal. The world stopped *tuning in*.

CHAPTER SEVEN

The Sincerity Trap

When Being Honest Still Isn't Enough

> *You shall not add to the word which I command you, nor take from it, that you may keep the commandments of the Lord your God which I command you.*
>
> — Deuteronomy 4:2

For the Israelites, it was just another desert morning. The camp stirred early. Fires crackled. Voices carried across the sand as people waited for something holy to happen. They were probably arguing over the last scraps of manna.

In the center of it all stood the tabernacle, still smelling of fresh linen and oil. Every inch designed by God. This was no human invention.

Inside, Aaron's sons, Nadab and Abihu, were preparing for worship.

These weren't amateurs. They'd seen the Red Sea split open. They'd eaten manna that fell from the sky. They stood at Sinai while the mountain burned because God was in the neighborhood. They knew what holiness looked like.

And still, they did something spectacularly dumb.

They lit the wrong fire.

> *Then Nadab and Abihu, the sons of Aaron, each took his censer and put fire in it, put incense on it, and offered profane fire before the Lord, which He had not commanded them. So fire went out from the Lord and devoured them, and they died before the Lord.*
>
> — Leviticus 10:1-2

Two priests. Two censers. One fatal assumption.

The fire was fast and final. Not metaphorical, not poetic, not some soft "learning experience."

To modern ears, the punishment sounds excessive. They were trying, right? They offered incense—something reverent. They weren't worshiping idols. They weren't building a golden calf.

They were worshiping the right God, just... freestyling the method.

> *By those who come near Me I must be regarded as holy; and before all the people I must be glorified.*
>
> — Leviticus 10:3

Nadab and Abihu assumed God's holiness was flexible—that sincerity was good enough, that their offering, if heartfelt, would be acceptable. But the text is clear: God didn't explicitly *ban* that fire. It wasn't *commanded.*

To Him, it was "profane fire."
Unauthorized.

Now compare that to Noah.

God gave him dimensions, materials, rooms, pitch, a door, and a design. He didn't say, "Don't use pine," or "Don't use oak." He didn't need to.

Noah didn't survive because he was inventive. He survived because he was obedient. Noah understood that when God speaks, silence isn't permission to innovate; it's a boundary to respect.

Nadab and Abihu died because they improvised. God was not rejecting worship; He was rejecting their *invention* (1 Samuel 15:22). That's the line.

Obedience is not the enemy of faith, and it is not legalism. It is alignment.

People want a *Savior* but not a *Lord* (Luke 6:46; 1 John 3:24). They crave the comfort of belief without the constraint of obedience. But faith without obedience isn't faith at all. It's fantasy.

For Nadab and Abihu, the issue wasn't belief but submission. It cost them everything.

That distinction—between believing and obeying—runs like a live wire through Scripture. Touch it carelessly and you'll feel the current.

Somewhere between those burned censers and our modern pulpits, God's warning still hangs in the air:

Don't offer what I haven't commanded.

Then Simon himself also believed; and when he was baptized he continued with Philip, and was amazed, seeing the miracles and signs which were done.

— Acts 8:13

Not everyone who boards the Ark understands the Captain.

Some people like the arrangement. Dry floors. Predictable meals. No drowning.

Simon is such a man. He believed and was baptized.

This movement around him was spreading—fast, visible, undeniable—and Simon was right in the middle of it all. Close enough to see it. Close enough to feel it.

Still, he got it wrong.

Not by rejecting God, but by trying to leverage Him (Acts 8:18–19).

You can almost hear the thought forming: *What if I could wield that?*

Maybe for influence. Maybe for control. Maybe, even in his own mind, for something good.

It didn't feel like rebellion. It felt like opportunity.

So he reached for the oldest language in the world: money. Because money makes things move.

Peter doesn't even hesitate.

"Your heart is not right in the sight of God... For I see that you are poisoned by bitterness and bound by iniquity" (Acts 8:21, 23).

Not your enthusiasm. Not your proximity. Not even the fact that you were there when it happened.

Your heart.

Because you can enter the water, stand shoulder-to-shoulder with the right people, watch the Spirit move—and still think you're the one in charge.

The Ark is entered once. That's decisive. That's final.

But the people inside still have a will. They choose. They drift. They decide who's really in charge.

Simon wasn't outside the Ark throwing rocks. He was inside. He didn't try to jump off. He tried to rearrange the furniture.

When Peter called him out, fear followed.

"Pray... that none of these things come upon me" (Acts 8:24).

Did he truly repent?

We aren't told.

And maybe that's the point.

The real danger isn't always walking away. That's easy to see. Easy to condemn. Easy, at least on the surface, to avoid.

Sometimes the danger is staying on the Ark—

and quietly deciding that you are the one in control.

———◆○◆———

O Lord, I know the way of man is not in himself; It is not in man who walks to direct his own steps.
— Jeremiah 10:23

There's a place where sincerity stops working.

Scripture hits that point often, and when it does, it doesn't raise its voice. It doesn't negotiate. It simply stops speaking.

That silence messes with us.

We like commands. Commands are manageable. Do this. Don't do that. Red light, green light. At least you know where you stand. Even prohibitions are comforting. They tell us where the lines are.

But silence feels different. It feels like freedom. Open. Neutral. Almost friendly. Like God stepped out for coffee and left us in charge.

It's a trap.

In Scripture, silence isn't God forgetting to finish the sentence. He isn't pausing to see what we think. It's a full stop. He's done speaking.

Sincerity is great at telling you why you want to do something. It's terrible at explaining why you're allowed to.

The writer of Hebrews makes this point. Jesus is declared our High Priest. That's not poetic language; it's a legal claim. And legally, it shouldn't work. Under Moses, priests came from Levi. Jesus came from Judah. There's no verse that says, *"Priests may not come from Judah."*

Instead, the writer drops this line like a blade:

"For it is evident that our Lord arose from Judah, of which tribe Moses spoke nothing concerning priesthood" (Hebrews 7:14).

Moses spoke *nothing*. That nothing carried authority. It disqualified entire tribes. By naming one, He excluded the rest.

Silence wasn't an invitation to improvise. It was the boundary. Here, sincerity reaches its limit.

A person may sincerely desire to serve God. A church may sincerely want to honor Jesus. They can cry. Pray. Mean it with everything they've got.

But tears are not keys.

Sincerity cannot unlock a door God never opened.

Do not add to His words, Lest He rebuke you, and you be found a liar.
— Proverbs 30:6

Silence doesn't ask how we feel about it. It only asks whether we will respect it.

Good intentions are admirable. They just aren't authoritative.

Obedience isn't born from how strongly we feel about something. It's shaped by what God has said—and sometimes by what He hasn't.

If silence is not permission, then we are no longer as free as we thought.

What do we do when Scripture is silent? Do we fill in the gaps, or do we stop? Is the text a foundation to build on, or a boundary to respect?

One says, "If God hasn't *condemned* it, it's allowed." The other says, "If God hasn't *authorized* it, it's forbidden" (1 Corinthians 4:6).

They're polar opposites. And the wrong choice couldn't be more tragic.

One leads to clarity. The other leads to confusion, division, and a path God never paved.

Here is a question every Christian must answer:

Did God give us a pattern for His church, or did He leave us to improvise?

The answer shapes our worship, our doctrine, and the church we choose to belong to.

When God speaks, silence isn't permission. Silence is direction.

His commands, His boundaries, and His patterns were spoken for our good—not to restrict us, but to free us from the tyranny of our own wisdom.

When we treat God's silence as approval, we stop being followers. We become inventors.

The church was never called to innovate. It was called to keep. Keep the faith. Keep the pattern (2 Timothy 1:13). Keep His Word.

Heaven and earth will pass away, but not one syllable of His truth will fail (Luke 16:17).

His Word will endure.

Whether we endure with it is another matter.

The final authority is either God's Word or our own.

It cannot be both.

CHAPTER EIGHT

The Closed Source

Who Gets to Change the Rules

> *If you believe what you like in the gospels, and reject what you don't like, it is not the gospel you believe, but yourself.*
> — Augustine of Hippo

At 2:25 p.m. on a Monday afternoon in 1990, the AT&T system collapsed.[1]

No bomb.
No hacker.
No enemy.

An engineer, competent and well-intentioned, made a small improvement. He didn't replace the system. He didn't dismantle its architecture. He added a patch: a minor tweak meant to make the network more efficient.

That tweak triggered an avalanche.

One switch reset itself. When it came back online, it signaled that everything was fine. Neighbors trusted it and rerouted traffic.

They crashed. When rebooted, they repeated the same lie. Within minutes, the network began eating itself alive.

New York went dark.
Then Chicago.
Then the East Coast.

Air traffic control couldn't place calls. Banks froze mid-transaction. Seventy-five million calls dissolved into static. The failure wasn't dramatic. It was orderly. Courteous. Systematic.

The network didn't collapse because someone rebelled against its design. It collapsed because someone assumed the design could absorb improvement. The engineer believed the system was flexible enough to accommodate his insight.

The network trusted itself.

That trust became a suicide pact.

> *Beloved, while I was very diligent to write to you concerning our common salvation, I found it necessary to write to you exhorting you to contend earnestly for the faith which was once for all delivered to the saints.*
>
> — Jude 1:3

We live in a world that loves updates.

Phones update overnight. Applications update weekly. Even our refrigerators want to update now, which feels excessive, but here we are.

We've absorbed the quiet assumption that nothing is ever really finished—that every system improves with iteration, and legitimacy belongs to whoever shows up with a better idea.

Authority only matters if it has limits.

Once something is truly authoritative, it's no longer experimental. It is no longer flexible. It is no longer open to negotiation by its users.

Christianity doesn't present itself as something unfinished.

It isn't modular.
It isn't versioned.
It isn't crowdsourced.

It arrives complete.

Alter it even slightly, and the failure doesn't show up right away. It keeps running. It looks functional—for a while.

That's how closed systems break—quietly.

Here's where things get counterintuitive.

We assume precision is uptight. That flexibility is generous. That exactness signals insecurity.

We treat doctrine like a buffet. Take what nourishes. Leave what offends. Customize to taste. Call it maturity.

Scripture treats truth like mathematics. Change a single variable, and the answer is no longer "mostly right." It's completely wrong.

God doesn't require precision because He's insecure. He requires it because He doesn't bend.

Truth, once spoken, doesn't need revision (Psalm 119:160).

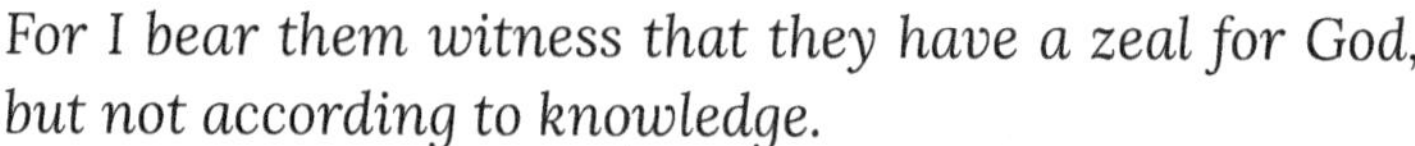

For I bear them witness that they have a zeal for God, but not according to knowledge.

— Romans 10:2

You can be sincere and still be inaccurate.

Take Apollos.

Acts describes him as eloquent, passionate, and mighty in the Scriptures. He was no amateur. He preached boldly about Jesus.

But his understanding stopped at the baptism of John.

The Resurrection had happened.
The covenant had shifted.
The message had advanced.

When Priscilla and Aquila heard him, they didn't clap politely. They didn't say, "Well, that's his truth." They didn't excuse it because his heart was in the right place.

They corrected him.

Luke uses a precise phrase: *more accurately* (Acts 18:26).

Those words matter. Accuracy assumes a fixed reference point. Correction assumes deviation. And deviation only exists if the system itself is settled.

If Christianity were an open system, Apollos wasn't wrong—he was just running a different build.

But Scripture doesn't flatter him like that. It calls him inaccurate.

Even the gifted submit.
Even the brilliant recalibrate.
Even the loudest voices don't get to redefine the signal.

———————◆○◆———————

But even if we, or an angel from heaven, preach any other gospel to you than what we have preached to you, let him be accursed. As we have said before, so now I say again, if anyone preaches any other gospel to you than what you have received, let him be accursed.
— Galatians 1:8–9

This is where Scripture refuses to behave like software.

Paul doesn't treat the gospel as a platform waiting for updates. He doesn't say, "Improve it carefully. Make it more... user-friendly. If the new version keeps the spirit of the original, we're fine."

He doesn't play that game. If anyone brings another gospel, reject it. He talks like a courier who's been told, "Don't open the package. Don't adjust the contents. Don't get creative. Just deliver it."

That is a closed door. A closed source (Deuteronomy 12:32).

We don't mind being fans. We don't mind contributing. We just want a hand on the wheel.

Christianity does not give us editorial control. We are the ones holding the envelope.

A steward guards what he's received. A servant carries what he's been given. A messenger repeats what he was sent to say.

None of them rewrite it (2 John 9).

And that feels... restrictive.

The question isn't whether a change feels useful, compassionate, modern, or sincere. The question is simpler:

Who owns the gospel?

If the apostles delivered the foundation, then we're not free to pour another one beside it. If Jesus is the cornerstone, then we're not free to move the walls because the room feels narrow.

Small edits don't stay small (2 Timothy 1:13).

They stack.

A tweak becomes a theme.
A theme becomes a doctrine.
A doctrine becomes a different church.

And a different church eventually offers a different gospel.

The gospel isn't a decorative feature of Christianity. It's the lifeboat. Change the message, and you don't make the lifeboat more welcoming.

You drill holes in the hull.

You either trust it—

or you drown.

For no other foundation can anyone lay than that which is laid, which is Jesus Christ.

— 1 Corinthians 3:11

This is where modern Christianity slips on wet pavement: we ask the wrong question.

Not: *What has God authorized?*
But: *What has He not forbidden?*

That question only makes sense in an open system where experimentation is expected.

Christianity isn't open source. The church wasn't released unfinished. Jesus didn't die to launch a think tank.

The cornerstone was set by Jesus. The foundation was laid by the apostles. The specs were delivered, not brainstormed (Ephesians 2:20).

We're not architects. We're custodians.

Our task is not innovation.

It is fidelity.

If anyone speaks, let him speak as the oracles of God.
— 1 Peter 4:11

There is an old rule from the Restoration Movement:

"Where the Scriptures speak, we speak. Where the Scriptures are silent, we're silent."

That rule sounds restrictive to modern ears.

It is.

But restriction isn't the enemy. It is the condition of survival in a closed system.

Pilots respect gravity.
Divers respect pressure.
Engineers respect tolerances.

Ignoring limits doesn't make you free. It makes you reckless.

Only fools demand freedom from reality.

Therefore we must give the more earnest heed to the things we have heard, lest we drift away.
— Hebrews 2:1

Drift is never dramatic. It feels thoughtful. Reasonable. Compassionate.

Once you decide the system is open, the edits never stop. *What did God say?* quietly becomes *What can we justify?*

And once that shift happens, drift is no longer accidental.

It's inevitable.

What remains may still resemble the Ark. It may even float—for a time. But it is no longer the vessel God designed to carry His people through the storm.

Closed systems don't adapt. They execute their logic.

The system doesn't belong to us.

The code isn't ours to change.

CHAPTER NINE

The Embassy

Living Somewhere You Don't Belong

> *Now therefore, if you will indeed obey My voice and keep My covenant, then you shall be a special treasure to Me above all people; for all the earth is Mine. And you shall be to Me a kingdom of priests and a holy nation. These are the words which you shall speak to the children of Israel.*
>
> — Exodus 19:5–6

Take a walk down Embassy Row in D.C. The air smells like diesel, sweat, and ambition. Everybody is going somewhere. The noise is a constant argument between traffic and language.

Then you turn a corner—and something's off.

Same street. Same noise. Same cracked sidewalk and impatient horns. But above the gate, snapping in the wind, is a flag that doesn't belong here. Wrong colors. Wrong symbols. Wrong story.

You could pass it a hundred times and never think twice. Until you try to enter.

Then everything changes.

A guard steps forward. Calm. Polite. Professional. You begin explaining yourself. People always do. But explanations don't open gates.

Credentials do.

Embassies don't run on sincerity. They run on authorization. You don't talk your way past the gate. Entrance is granted, not improvised.

Local laws slow down at the curb and die at the gate. Inside the fence, a foreign government operates with authority that didn't originate here.

This is how the New Testament describes the church.

Our citizenship is in heaven (Philippians 3:20). We are sojourners and pilgrims (1 Peter 2:11). And the Kingdom we belong to isn't of this world (John 18:36)—no matter how badly we want it to be.

These aren't metaphors meant to soften the message. They're meant to sharpen it.

The church doesn't draw authority from culture.
Its legitimacy doesn't come from popularity.
Its boundaries aren't drawn by a show of hands.

Like an embassy, it operates by charter: who gets in, how they enter, and what loyalty looks like.

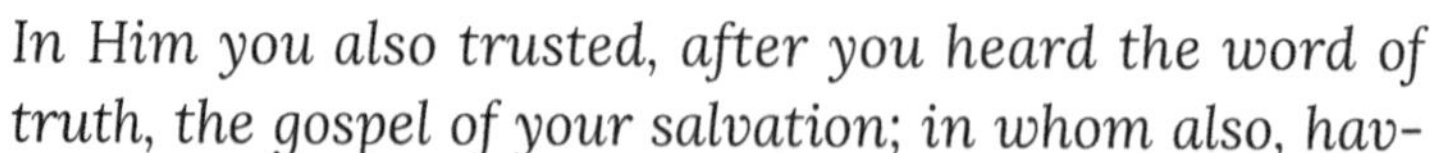

In Him you also trusted, after you heard the word of truth, the gospel of your salvation; in whom also, hav-

*ing believed, you were sealed with the Holy Spirit of
promise.*

— Ephesians 1:13

How do you prove you belong inside the gate?

In the modern world, we use biometrics and holograms. In the ancient world, they used clay.

Beneath the limestone rubble south of Jerusalem's Temple Mount, archaeologists uncovered something easy to miss: a small lump of clay, hardened by fire and time, no larger than a fingernail. To the naked eye, it looked like dirt. Ordinary. Disposable.

Until they cleaned it.

Pressed into its surface, written in Paleo-Hebrew, were words that refused to fade:

"Belonging to Hezekiah, son of Ahaz, King of Judah."[1]

That tiny seal once secured a royal document. It marked ownership, authority, and authenticity. The palace is gone. The king is dust. The empire is a footnote.

But the seal still speaks across three millennia.

"This belongs to the King."

That's what a seal does. It doesn't argue or persuade.

It declares.

Paul uses the same word to describe Christians. Not merely inspired. Not merely encouraged.

Sealed.

A seal is not a feeling. It's a mark of ownership applied by authority. No one seals themselves. And no seal exists without a sovereign hand to press it.

This is the church: not a crowd of spiritual consumers, but a people marked as belonging to Another (1 Peter 2:9).

Recognized. Authorized.

The Lord knows those who are His.

— 2 Timothy 2:19

Ask the average person what a church is, and they'll point to a building. A steeple. Rows of pews. A cross standing guard out front. That answer would have baffled the first Christians.

You could bulldoze every one of those buildings and the church wouldn't have a scratch on it.

When Paul wrote to believers scattered across the Roman world, he used a word drawn from civic life:

Ekklesia.

A called-out assembly. Citizens summoned to act on behalf of the city.

Paul didn't pick that word by accident. You are not a religious club. You're a government in exile, a living body operating behind enemy lines (2 Corinthians 5:20).

Somewhere between Pentecost and PowerPoint, we forgot this. The church became a place we go instead of a people we are.

Embassies aren't community centers or cultural exchange programs.

They exist to represent their King.

For our citizenship is in heaven, from which we also eagerly wait for the Savior, the Lord Jesus Christ...
— Philippians 3:20

When did this embassy open?

The prophets saw it coming. Isaiah spoke of a mountain to which the nations would stream (Isaiah 2:2). Daniel saw a Kingdom that would never be destroyed (Daniel 2:44). But the charter took effect on a specific day.

Pentecost.

Jerusalem was crowded with pilgrims from every corner of the empire. Languages collided. Cultures overlapped. And in the middle of that chaos, God didn't send a memo.

He sent wind.

Days earlier, these men were hiding behind locked doors. Now they were in the street, speaking languages they had never learned to people who had no reason to understand them. Parthians. Medes. Elamites. Strangers suddenly hearing heaven in their own tongue.

They had come for a feast and walked into a charter event.

Not a manifesto. A message.

God's dwelling was no longer confined to stone. The law, once carved into tablets, was moving into human hearts.

The embassy opened its doors at last.

And the Lord added to the church daily those who were being saved.

— Acts 2:47

Acts never talks about people *joining* the church. That's our language.

Modern. Corporate. Transactional.

In the New Testament, the Lord adds. No committee. No membership card.

You don't join the church like a gym. You're born into it, recognized by the King who owns it (John 3:5).

Which makes the real question unavoidable.

Not, "Have you joined a church?"
But, "Has the Lord added you to His?"

He's the One who keeps the registry.

For through Him we both have access in one Spirit to the Father.

— Ephesians 2:18

An embassy doesn't care how badly you want protection. It only recognizes those whose names are on record.

If you aren't recognized by the King, you're outside. You may admire the building and quote its laws. You may stand at the gate and argue your case until your voice gives out.

But admiration isn't asylum. Proximity isn't protection.

Safety is found beneath a seal pressed by His authority.

"This belongs to the King."

Chapter Ten

The Fugazi

The Lie That Feels Most Like Truth

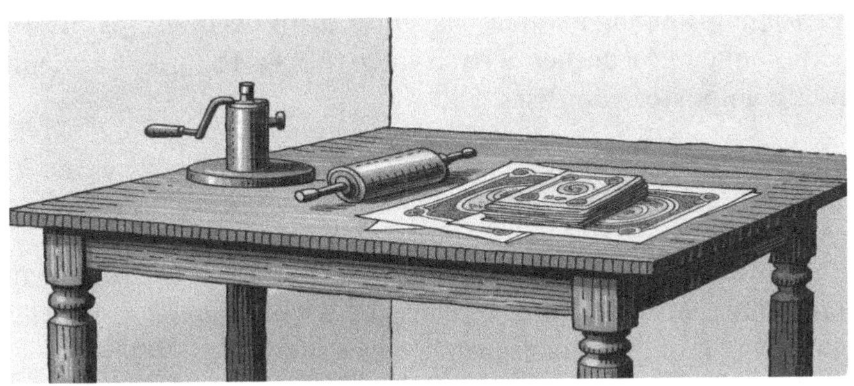

> *Test all things; hold fast what is good.*
>
> — 1 Thessalonians 5:21

At the Federal Reserve Bank in Boston—a money monastery—a small team of experts processes an average of 5.2 million banknotes every day. They sort America's wallet. Every crumpled Washington. Every sweaty Jackson.

This isn't glamorous work.

Their mission is to ensure the blood of the economy is genuine. Machines manage a river of currency, scanning paper fiber and magnetic ink at warp speed.

But everyone in the room knows the truth: the final referee isn't the tech.

It's human.[1]

A trained eye. A familiar touch.

That trained eye isn't folklore. It's a job description. Some examiners can spot a fake blindfolded. Not because they memorized every trick in the playbook, but because they've handled real money so long that anything else feels off.

It isn't magic. It's familiarity.

Years spent flipping genuine bills until truth becomes instinct—a tactile language of authenticity. Handle the real thing long enough, and the impostor confesses.

Counterfeiters, of course, have evolved. They always do (2 Corinthians 11:14).

Forget the old print shop in the garage. Today's pros create "supercounterfeits." They bleach genuine one-dollar bills—*literally* laundering money—then reprint them as hundreds.

Same paper. Same fibers. Same smell. Most people can't tell the difference.

The experts at the Fed don't stare at fakes all day. They barely look at them.

The secret to spotting a lie isn't becoming fluent in lies. It's becoming so saturated in truth that lies offend you. The genuine article becomes your native language.

Everything else sounds like gibberish.

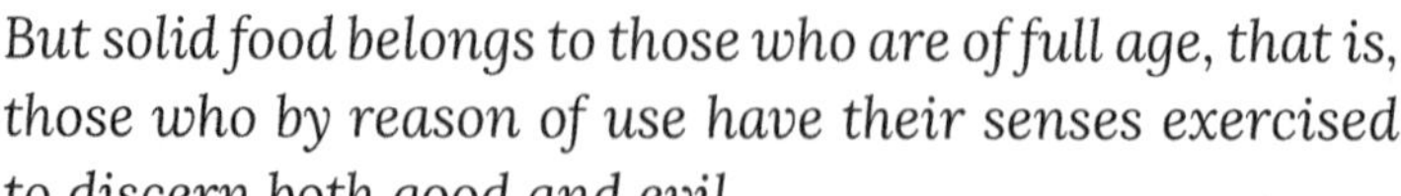

But solid food belongs to those who are of full age, that is, those who by reason of use have their senses exercised to discern both good and evil.

— Hebrews 5:14

Step outside the Fed, however, and the standard drops.

A local news story recently warned about a wave of fake bills hitting small businesses.[2] These weren't master forgeries produced by criminal syndicates. They were "prop bills." Movie money. Hollywood leftovers.

They weren't even pretending to be authentic.

Instead of *The United States of America*, the banner screams FOR MOTION PICTURE USE ONLY. Instead of the Treasurer's signature, it says *Prop Master*. And where *In God We Trust* should be, the bills read: *In Prop We Trust*.[3]

The truth wasn't hidden. It was printed in bold, right there on the face. And yet people used them anyway. And others accepted them (2 Timothy 4:4).

Because we're like that.

The outline was right.
The color was close.
The feel was familiar.

And that was enough.

In court, juries are told that a counterfeit doesn't have to be perfect. It only has to fool someone exercising "ordinary caution."[4]

Translation: close is close enough (Matthew 7:22–23).

Counterfeiters rely on distraction, not genius. They count on us to be busy, trusting, and unwilling to slow down long enough to look closely. Close enough is how fraud survives. It circulates. It destroys.

"Close enough," as it turns out, is the devil's favorite phrase.

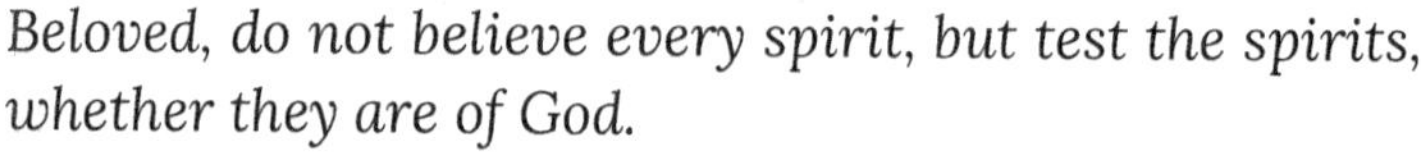

*Beloved, do not believe every spirit, but test the spirits,
whether they are of God.*

— 1 John 4:1

We live in an era of spiritual prop money.

There are churches built for "motion picture use only." Perfect
lighting. Perfect playlists. Perfect slogans. From the street, it all
looks legit. Inside, the mood hits just right (2 Timothy 3:5).

But slow down and read the inscription.

The authority is different.
The signature is missing.
The seal doesn't match.

We get fooled because we're distracted. We accept spiritual currency in circulation because it looks and feels right.

Counterfeits need speed. They need you to be busy and unwilling
to look closely.

They only need to survive long enough to change hands.

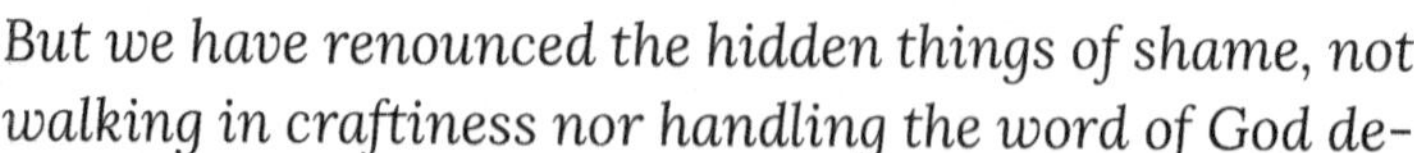

*But we have renounced the hidden things of shame, not
walking in craftiness nor handling the word of God de-*

ceitfully, but by manifestation of the truth commending ourselves to every man's conscience in the sight of God.
— 2 Corinthians 4:2

Here's the funny thing about truth.

Truth is heavy, inconvenient, and quiet. It sits in your hand without trying to impress you.

Counterfeits, on the other hand, are always performing. They have no intrinsic value, so they survive on momentum.

People think the way to avoid deception is to study the heretics. To memorize every scam. But that's not how discernment works.

You don't study the darkness to find the light. You study the light until the darkness becomes obvious (John 10:4–5).

That's how the Fed trains its people. Handle the real thing long enough, and the fakes can't hide.

Scripture trains us the same way. When the church Jesus built becomes second nature, impostors can't hide. They may be sincere. They may even be moving. They are still not the genuine article.

A bill only has value if it bears the mark of the Treasury. A life only has weight if it bears the seal of the Spirit (Romans 8:16).

The world is full of "In Prop We Trust."

The genuine article bears a different inscription.

Not in polish.
Not in performance.
Not in props.

In God We Trust.

And a counterfeit, no matter how beautiful, cannot pay your debt.

CHAPTER ELEVEN

The Driftwood

Why Some Things Survive That Shouldn't

> *There is one body and one Spirit, just as you were called in one hope of your calling; one Lord, one faith, one baptism; one God and Father of all, who is above all, and through all, and in you all.*
>
> — Ephesians 4:4–6

We like to think disaster arrives without warning. Sudden. Random. Impossible to see coming.

But in 1666, the Great Fire of London wasn't an accident. It was inevitable.

London's greatest asset—the extreme density that drove its global commerce—was also its greatest threat. In every alley, timber was stacked for trade. Chimneys spat sparks into the sky so thick with coal smoke you could chew it. The sight of sparks dancing over a thousand wooden roofs should have inspired a little caution.

It didn't.

After the fire, Londoners were desperate for protection. Naturally, insurance companies stepped up. Fire insurance became the city's newest obsession.

But there was a problem.

There were no municipal fire departments.

So insurance companies filled the void with private brigades.[1] Those crews had one mission: save the paying customer. To keep things organized, they bolted metal plaques bearing company logos to houses. A sun. A lion. A castle.

When fire broke out, the brigades rushed to the scene. Amid smoke and shouting, they didn't look for the flames.

They looked for the plaque.

If the house had the right logo on the wall, they fought the fire. If it didn't, they stood back and watched it burn.

Choice, it turns out, didn't guarantee rescue. It merely identified who belonged to whom. When your house is on fire, you don't want options.

You want water.

> But I will establish My covenant with you; and you shall go into the ark.
>
> — Genesis 6:18

Now zoom out.

In matters of faith, our world is overflowing with "Ark competitors." Ancient ones. Modern ones. Some carved from tradition. Others assembled from innovation and personal conviction. All built by human hands. All swear they float.

We assume more religious choice means more safety. That's a comforting lie. Scripture tells a different story.

Noah's task wasn't creativity. It was obedience. God gave him a design, a door, a vessel. Dimensions. Materials. Rooms. Pitch. A blueprint for survival (Genesis 6:14–16).

We *can* build boats. That was never in doubt. The issue is whether God sanctified more than one.

We like diversification. Keep your options open. Spread the risk. In finance, that advice keeps you solvent. In faith, it drowns you.

God isn't managing a portfolio. According to Paul, every spiritual blessing is found in one place: in Christ (Ephesians 1:3). Redemption. Reconciliation. Life. All of it. No backup plan.

That's why Paul's list in Ephesians matters. One body. One Spirit. One hope. One Lord. One faith. One baptism. One God and Father (Ephesians 4:4–6).

Baptism keeps serious company. Paul places it right next to faith—not in the margins, not among optional add-ons, not somewhere down the hallway after salvation has already happened. Right there. Beside Lordship. Beside the body itself.

God does not franchise salvation across competing models.

He builds one house, names the terms, and opens the door.

—◦—

For as the body is one and has many members, but all the members of that one body, being many, are one body, so also is Christ.

— 1 Corinthians 12:12

How, then, did we move from one body to endless division?

Part of the answer is linguistic decay. Lawyers call it *genericide,* the gradual loss of precision when a name is used so often it goes soft.[2]

We call them "denominations." The very word assumes division—different names for what was meant to be one.

The word *Christian* suffered this fate.

In Acts, that word was dangerous (Acts 11:26). Probably an insult. It described people whose allegiance to Jesus reordered their lives. It cost them reputation. Safety. Sometimes blood.

It meant something because it demanded something.

Today, the word is elastic. It can mean your grandparents. Your voting habits. Your Christmas decorations. It can be claimed without obedience and worn without transformation.

When a name grows weak, we try to sharpen it. Qualifiers start appearing. Hyphens multiply.

"I am a *something*-Christian."

But the first disciples didn't need qualifiers. The name was big enough to swallow every other allegiance they had.

Prefixes create distinctions that were meant to be surrendered.

Unless the Lord builds the house, they labor in vain who build it.

— Psalm 127:1

Here's the harder one.

Some denominations started with good intentions. Someone saw corruption and wanted reform. Someone saw drift and wanted correction. That's how it almost always begins.

Concern.
Conviction.
A new structure.

We think God's design needs our input. A little tweak here. A doctrinal patch there. Just in case.

But the Ark wasn't fragile. The pattern wasn't incomplete.

Sincerity does not sanctify what God did not authorize.

Jeremiah saw this psychology play out long ago.

"My people have committed two evils," God said.
"They have forsaken Me, the fountain of living waters, and hewn themselves cisterns—broken cisterns that can hold no water" (Jeremiah 2:13).

A fountain flows without management.

A cistern requires our hands.

We like engineered things because they feel manageable and adjustable. When cracks appear, we patch them. Yet every human system eventually leaks.

When a drought comes, the problem isn't water.

It's the *container*.

The fountain never stopped flowing. We simply trusted our own plumbing more.

Nor is there salvation in any other, for there is no other name under heaven given among men by which we must be saved.

— Acts 4:12

The Flood didn't care if you believed your driftwood would float. It revealed what could carry life—and what could not.

The Ark had one door (Genesis 6:16). Every life that passed through it was saved the same way.

Jesus does not have competing bodies. He does not maintain rival houses under different names. He is not asking us to improve the vessel or diversify the rescue.

Useful is not the same as authorized.

What matters is whether God built it.

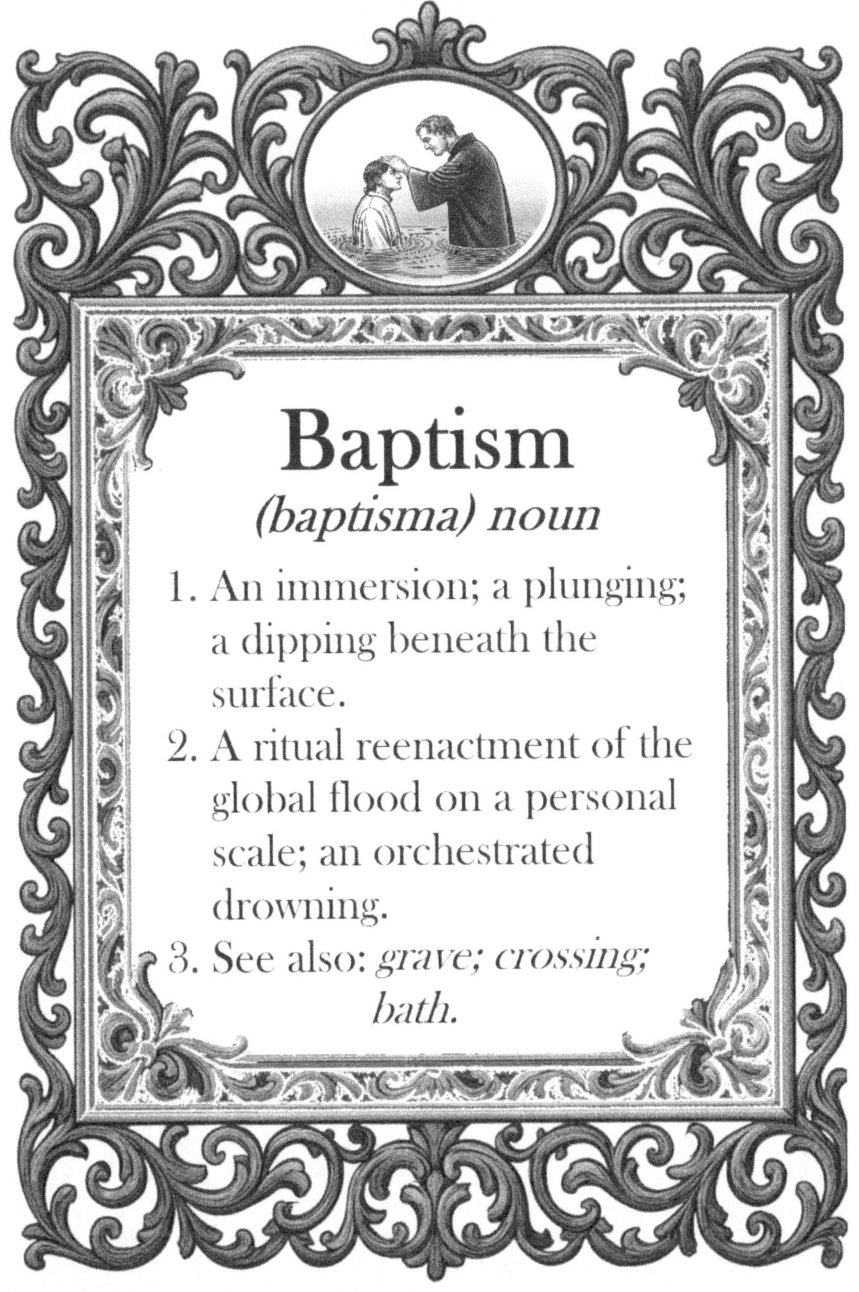

Baptism
(baptisma) noun

1. An immersion; a plunging;
a dipping beneath the
surface.

2. A ritual reenactment of the
global flood on a personal
scale; an orchestrated
drowning.

3. See also: grave; crossing;
bath.

CHAPTER TWELVE

The Cosmic Mikvah

The Line You Don't Come Back Across

> *Who may ascend into the hill of the Lord? Or who may stand in His holy place? He who has clean hands and a pure heart, who has not lifted up his soul to an idol, nor sworn deceitfully.*
>
> — Psalm 24:3–4

P urity isn't about being perfect. It's about being precise.

There's a room at NASA's Goddard Space Flight Center that feels less like a laboratory and more like a temple. Before you can enter, you pass through a series of rituals. Shoes covered. Gloves sealed. Body wrapped in layers of synthetic fabric.

You stand still while filtered air blasts over you, stripping away invisible specks of dust. Inside, the air is replaced dozens of times each minute. Every movement is slow. Deliberate.

This isn't about hygiene. It is reverence disguised as engineering.

This is where the James Webb Space Telescope was assembled—humanity's most sensitive eye, angled toward creation itself.[1]

Each gold-coated mirror is so finely tuned that a single fleck of dust could scatter light and blur distant galaxies.

Billions of dollars. Decades of genius. And the whole thing could be ruined by a tiny fleck of dandruff.

The engineers understand something ancient: when precision meets presence, preparation isn't optional. You don't approach what is sacred casually. You slow down. You cleanse. You make space for light to arrive undistorted.

> *I will wash my hands in innocence; so I will go about*
> *Your altar, O Lord.*
>
> — Psalm 26:6

In a sense, Israel's Tabernacle was the universe's first clean room.

If you trace your finger through the pages of the Old Testament, a pattern emerges. Whenever God draws near, water appears.

Priests washed, Levites washed, the people washed before Sinai. Those who touched death or disease washed before rejoining the camp. And before Israel ever heard God's voice, they were commanded to wash themselves and their garments (Exodus 19:10–11, 14–15; 30:17–21; Joshua 3:14–17).

Water marks approach.

At the heart of Israel's sacrificial worship stood a bronze basin, placed between the altar and the tent of meeting. It didn't look like much: no carvings, no jewels, no spectacle. Just water, waiting.

Its purpose, however, was unmistakable. Its logic was severe.

You couldn't wander into the presence of God smelling of goat and campfire. You paused. You prepared. You washed. The instruction was blunt: "They must wash... so that they may not die."

This wasn't hygiene. It was a threshold.

The basin wasn't a sink. It was a checkpoint.

God set the terms of approach. The water had no power on its own. It mattered because God placed it at the threshold and attached His command to it.

Holiness wasn't a suggestion. It was lethal.

And the higher you went, the more precise the washing became.

On the Day of Atonement, the holiest day of the year, the High Priest washed, entered the veil, completed the ritual, and washed again before returning to the people (Leviticus 16:4, 23–24).

The message was absolute: you don't cross between realms casually.

That you may distinguish between holy and unholy, and between unclean and clean.

— Leviticus 10:10

Anthropologists call these washings *boundary rituals*[2]—the moment you cross from one state of being to another, where the rules of the ordinary world no longer apply.

In the ancient imagination, dirt was never just dirt. It was matter out of place—a small, physical form of chaos. Washing, then, wasn't cosmetic. It was corrective.

Scripture calls it something far more direct.

Preparation.

The water didn't make them clean—not in the way that mattered. It made them ready.

Because in Scripture, water was never neutral. It was a gift and a threat. Cleansing and chaos. Life and judgment (Genesis 6–8; Exodus 14).

Which is why the Bible does not begin with a garden. It begins with water (Genesis 1:2).

The Spirit hovers over chaos and brings order. Light from darkness. Boundary from flood. A world made habitable by His Word. That pattern never disappears.

The *mikvah*, a ritual bath, emerged as an extension of this older truth: that approaching the Holy One requires intention, readiness, and a willing submission to order.

Water marked the boundary.

It marked the crossing (1 Corinthians 10:1–2; Hebrews 11:29).

Now the flood was on the earth forty days.
— Genesis 7:17

The rabbis reasoned that a proper mikvah couldn't be filled by hand. It had to contain *living water*—rain, spring, water untouched by human control.

Not any amount.

Forty *seah.*

Not forty-*ish*, but forty. Enough water to swallow a human body whole.

In Judaism, numbers are never just numbers. They are hyperlinks connecting one story to another.

Forty *seah* in the mikvah.
Forty days of rain in Noah's Flood.

This was no coincidence. To the rabbis, the Flood wasn't only an execution. It was a ritual—a cosmic mikvah for the entire planet.

The corruption was too ingrained to scrub out. It had to be reborn.

A convert steps into forty *seah* and comes out someone new.

The earth stepped into forty days and came out reborn.

Once you see the pattern of forty, it starts photobombing the whole Bible. Forty doesn't merely measure duration. It measures transformation. Moses on Sinai. Israel in the wilderness. Jesus in the desert.

You enter the forty as one thing.

You exit as another.

The Flood, then, was the original baptism, the first lesson God taught humanity in water:

Some things must go under to come up whole.

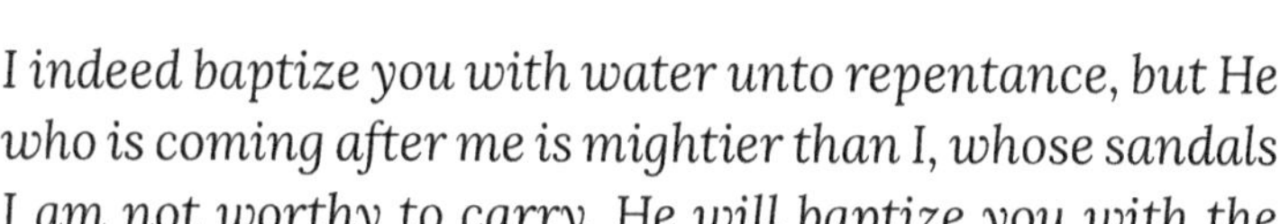

> *I indeed baptize you with water unto repentance, but He who is coming after me is mightier than I, whose sandals I am not worthy to carry. He will baptize you with the Holy Spirit and fire.*
>
> — Matthew 3:11

This is why the events at the Jordan mattered.

When John the Baptist appeared, he didn't set up shop in the Temple. He went to the river. The border. The place where Israel first crossed into promise (Joshua 3:14–17).

By dragging the nation back to the Jordan, John made a devastating claim: *You are not home.*

He was telling the chosen people that heritage wasn't enough. They needed to start again. To cross over again.

He wasn't offering a rinse.

He was calling for a reset.

The religious elite were not amused. The Pharisees arrived expecting deference. John treated them like outsiders. By refusing the water, they were rejecting the very plan God had designed to save the nation.

But the tax collectors came. So did the soldiers. So did the poor.

In the water, everyone's resume dissolves.

John knew his limits. "I baptize with water," he said, "but someone is coming with fire." John could change direction. He couldn't change hearts.

He held the lantern.

But he wasn't the dawn.

For John truly baptized with water, but you shall be baptized with the Holy Spirit not many days from now.
— Acts 1:5

The Jordan wasn't majestic. It was muddy. Moving. Unsettled. To the ancient mind, it carried the meaning of chaos—the same chaos God ordered at creation.

Then the unthinkable happened. Jesus came to the river and asked John to baptize Him.

John tried to refuse. Jesus insisted. *"Permit it to be so now, for thus it is fitting for us to fulfill all righteousness"* (Matthew 3:15).

Jesus didn't stand on the bank offering commentary. He stepped into the water and was immersed—not because He needed cleansing, but because He had come to bring order where chaos ruled.

As He rose from the river, heaven cracked open. The Spirit descended like a dove. The Father spoke.

Genesis opens with the Spirit hovering over water (Genesis 1:2). The Gospel opens with the Spirit descending over the Son in the river (Matthew 3:16).

Jesus wasn't merely identifying with sinners. He was announcing His mission.

And immediately, the chaos began to reverse. The blind saw. The lame walked. The poor heard good news. Bodies bent by sin were restored. Lives curved inward were straightened.

Jesus didn't avoid the chaos.

He entered it.

> But I have a baptism to be baptized with, and how distressed I am till it is accomplished!
>
> — Luke 12:50

We don't usually think of the crucifixion as baptismal.

But Jesus did.

Israel understood washing as preparation for approaching God. Before Sinai, before the priesthood, before the holy place, they entered the water. It prepared the whole person to enter His presence:

The head—your thoughts.
The heart—your desires.

The hands—your deeds.
The feet—your walk.

At the Cross, that pattern reaches unbearable clarity.

Thorns pressed into His head.
Nails pierced His hands and feet.
A spear opened His side, and blood and water flowed out.

Jesus gathered into His own body the places where sin lives. He bore the cost for all of it.

The crucifixion was not merely the price behind cleansing. It was the cleansing place itself.

His suffering became *the* baptism He spoke of.

Then there appeared to them divided tongues, as of fire, and one sat upon each of them.
— Acts 2:3

John's baptism wasn't Christian baptism.

Jesus claimed it to transform it from the inside, to fulfill it. He took the boundary ritual of the old world and turned it into the entrance ramp of the new.

When the crowds were baptized, they came up repentant.
When Jesus was baptized, He came up anointed.

John promised water.
Jesus promised fire.

The switch flipped.

The water was no longer only about washing away the past. It became the doorway to the power of the future—the Holy Spirit.

The people saw the first flicker of fire from heaven. And that's when everything became dangerous.

Because once fire finds a door, it doesn't just warm the room...

...it spreads.

Chapter Thirteen

The Caisson

What You Build Where No One Can See

> *He is like a man building a house, who dug deep and laid the foundation on the rock. And when the flood arose, the stream beat vehemently against that house, and could not shake it, for it was founded on the rock.*
>
> — Luke 6:48

There's a certain type of work that can't be done in the sunshine. Foundations are like this.

We admire massive skyscrapers, towers, and bridges. We name buildings after donors who never touched a shovel. Meanwhile, the actual work happens underground. It's in places that smell like rust and wet stone, where nobody is smiling for the camera.

When Washington Roebling set out to build the Brooklyn Bridge in 1869, he ran into a problem. He needed to raise massive stone towers to carry suspension cables. But beneath the East River lay nothing but soft, shifting silt. If he built on that, the bridge wouldn't just sag; it would collapse. Publicly. Catastrophically.

So, before he built up, he had to go down.

Roebling designed *caissons*—massive wooden boxes—and sank them into the river like coffins with a purpose. Teams of men, known as "sandhogs," climbed inside and descended into the dark. They left fresh air behind. Under insane pressure, they dug through mud, rot, and centuries of garbage. They were looking for one thing:

Bedrock.

The work was brutal. Gas lamps belched oily black smoke, coating everyone in a layer of soot. One worker called it *Dante's Inferno*—men sweating profusely in a dim hell, clawing through muck as if trying to reach the underworld by hand. Some got the bends. Some didn't come back at all. It crippled Roebling. He was forced to watch his bridge rise through a telescope from his bedroom window.[1]

Once the workers hit rock, they filled the caissons with concrete and buried them forever.

No plaque.
No credit.
Just silence.

That's how foundations work (1 Corinthians 3:11).

John the Baptist was a spiritual sandhog.

He wasn't the bridge or the tower. He didn't claim to be the destination. He was deep in the caisson of the heart, scraping away self-justification, religious posturing, and spiritual cosplay.

John didn't build a thing. He cleared the ground (Isaiah 40:3).

That mattered, because you can't build a life on mud. Eventually, the flood shows up (Matthew 7:26–27). It always does. And whatever looked "nice enough" on a sunny day folds like wet cardboard when the water rises.

But digging has limits.

A caisson isn't a house. You don't live there. You don't grow there. Repentance works the same way: it clears space, but it doesn't create life (Ezekiel 36:25–27; Jeremiah 2:22). Living perpetually in confession isn't holiness.

It's paralysis.

There's a real danger in learning to love the mud.[2]

That's why the project changes when Jesus arrives.

John digs down.

Jesus builds up.

There was a man of the Pharisees named Nicodemus, a ruler of the Jews.

— John 3:1

The first man to trip over this new blueprint wasn't some skeptic. He was an expert.

Nicodemus had serious credentials. Pharisee. Ruler. Law savant. If religion were a bureaucracy, this guy would have tenure and a reserved parking spot. He understood the mechanics well: keep the rules, perform the rituals, keep your hands clean. To him, the covenant was pure genetics. You were born a Jew, you lived as a Jew, and you died a Jew. Kingdom membership by Abraham's bloodline.

Still, something was missing.

Nicodemus came to Jesus at night (John 3:2). That's when experts ask questions they're afraid to ask in daylight.

Jesus didn't flatter him. He said something that sounded impossible:

"Unless one is born again, he cannot see the kingdom of God" (John 3:3).

Nicodemus heard "born" and thought biology. Surely God renovates what already exists.

So he asked the obvious question. Jesus cut through it:

"Unless one is born of water and the Spirit, he cannot enter the kingdom of God" (John 3:5).

Jesus joined water and Spirit in one birth. Same sentence. Same movement. Same doorway. We may try to pry them apart, but Jesus didn't hand Nicodemus two keys and tell him to pick his favorite.

This wasn't a tune-up. It was total replacement.

Water can wash you. It can tell the truth about your dirt. But water, by itself, can't make you alive (John 6:63; Titus 3:5). The Spirit does that. It's the difference between repainting a collapsing barn and building a new one from the ground up.

Nicodemus thought renovation.

Jesus spoke new construction.

The gospel isn't about making bad people better.

It's about making dead people alive (1 Peter 1:23).

You can be good and still unborn.

This is where things go wrong.

People turn belief into a permanent construction site—digging forever, confessing forever, apologizing forever. Always tearing down. Never letting anything stand. Living like the hole is the house.

The soul can't survive on demolition alone (Hebrews 6:1).

Digging is essential.

It is not sufficient.

Jesus, knowing that the Father had given all things into His hands, and that He had come from God and was going to God, rose from supper and laid aside His garments, took a towel and girded Himself.

— John 13:3–4

On the night before the crucifixion, Jesus does something that looks like a contradiction.

The disciples are arguing. The world's grime is still on their feet. Jesus takes a towel, kneels, and starts washing.

Peter objects. "You shall never wash my feet!"

Jesus answers, "If I do not wash you, you have no part with Me."

Peter swings hard the other way. "Lord, not my feet only, but also my hands and my head!"

He wanted another baptism. Another caisson. Another foundation pour.

Jesus stopped him.

"He who is bathed needs only to wash his feet, but is completely clean" (John 13:8–10).

That sentence changes everything.

Foundations happen once. You don't repour concrete every time it rains. But you do clean off the dirt you pick up walking through the world.

In baptism, God builds the house.

Repentance keeps it livable (1 John 1:7–9).

> *But you are not in the flesh but in the Spirit, if indeed the Spirit of God dwells in you. Now if anyone does not have the Spirit of Christ, he is not His.*
>
> — Romans 8:9

Years later, Paul arrives in Ephesus and finds twelve "disciples" who missed the memo. They look right. Talk right. But something's off.

Paul asks a probing question: "Did you receive the Holy Spirit when you believed?"

They blink. "We haven't even heard there's a Holy Spirit."

Paul checks their paperwork. "Into what then were you baptized?"

"John's baptism."

There it is.

John's baptism was a caisson. Temporary. Necessary. Expired (Acts 19:4-5). Its sell-by date was the Resurrection. Pentecost changed the terms.

That earlier baptism looked forward. Christian baptism looks back—to the finished death, burial, and resurrection of Jesus. One prepared Israel for what was coming. The other belongs to the age after the Cross, after the Resurrection, and after Pentecost.

Paul doesn't shrug and say, "Well, your heart was in the right place." He baptizes them again—this time into the name of Jesus.

Why?

Because precision matters. This isn't legalism; it's engineering. If you build on the wrong foundation, the flood still wins. A person can be sincere and still be wrong.

Reality doesn't care how much you "meant well" (Proverbs 14:12; Romans 10:2).

All authority has been given to Me in heaven and on earth.

— Matthew 28:18

After the Resurrection, Jesus met His disciples on a mountain and gave them His final marching orders. The debate was over. No more digging. No more prep work. The caisson was laid—in His blood.

For centuries, access to God depended on location and lineage. A place you could point to. A family tree you could trace. Jesus retired all of it.

Go.
Make disciples.
Baptize.
Teach them to observe everything He commanded (Matthew 28:19–20).

Not into a tribe.
Not into a tradition.
But into a Name (Acts 4:12).

Water with Spirit. Obedience fused to birth. Submission joined to adoption. That's what Nicodemus couldn't see in the dark: the foundation was never the goal. It was preparation for the life that would be built on top of it.

The blueprint was set. The excavation was over. It was time to stop digging and start living.

So they went back to Jerusalem and waited.

They had the water.
They had the command.

They just needed the fire (Acts 1:4–5).

CHAPTER FOURTEEN

The Glass Floor

The Step You Still Haven't Taken

> Trust in the Lord with all your heart, and lean not on your own understanding; in all your ways acknowledge Him, and He shall direct your paths.
>
> — Proverbs 3:5–6

There are certain experiences that show us what we actually believe.

The Grand Canyon Skywalk sounds simple until you're standing on it. It's a horseshoe of glass suspended 4,000 feet above the canyon floor.

Engineers will tell you that it can hold the weight of seventy-one 747s. Constructed from reinforced steel and layered glass, it can withstand gale-force winds.[1] Statistically speaking, you're safer on that bridge than in the parking lot you just crossed.

And yet, when people reach the edge, something happens.

They freeze.

You see it in the videos. Visitors step forward and glance down. Knees wobble. A nervous laugh. They believe the bridge exists. They just don't trust it with their body.

The thing is, you can't experience the Skywalk from the railing. At some point, you've got to put your weight on the glass and let gravity negotiate.

Belief waits at the edge. Faith steps forward (2 Corinthians 5:7).

Scripture is full of people who had to do the exact same thing.

Has the Lord as great delight in burnt offerings and sacrifices, as in obeying the voice of the Lord? Behold, to obey is better than sacrifice, and to heed than the fat of rams.

— 1 Samuel 15:22

In 2 Kings 5, we meet Naaman. He was the commander of the Syrian army.

He was a man who had everything: a general, a war hero, powerful and wealthy. If a problem could be conquered, he was the one to do it.

But beneath his confidence was the quiet ruin of leprosy, a humiliating enemy that refused to bow.

When he heard there was a prophet in Israel who could heal him, he showed up ready to impress. He brought silver, gold, and a whole new wardrobe. He expected a reception that matched his status. He wanted a prophet who'd recognize importance when he saw it.

Instead, Elisha didn't even come to the door. He sent a messenger out with a single sentence that sounded like a prank: "Go and wash in the Jordan seven times, and your flesh shall be restored to you, and you shall be clean" (2 Kings 5:10).

No lightning bolts.
No spectacle.
Just river water.

Naaman was furious.

If you're a powerful man with a serious disease, you expect a serious solution. He'd traveled hundreds of miles for a miracle and ended up with a chore.

The Jordan? Please. It's unimpressive, muddy, rural. "Are not Abanah and Pharpar, the rivers of Damascus, better than all the waters of Israel?" he snapped. Why would the God of Israel choose such a dull way to show grace?

Pride doesn't mind difficulty. Pride minds simplicity.

His servants, the unsung heroes of this story, talked some sense into him: if the prophet had told you to do something hard, wouldn't you have done it? Why refuse this simple thing?

So Naaman stepped into the river.

He dipped once. Twice. By the fifth dip, he probably felt ridiculous. Six, still leprous. But something inside him began to shift. With each dip, his pride slowly dissolved until there was nothing left but surrender.

On the seventh dip, he came up clean (2 Kings 5:14).

Naaman didn't get healed because the water was magical—he was healed because he did what he was told.

Faith is not good intentions. Faith is finishing what God said to do.

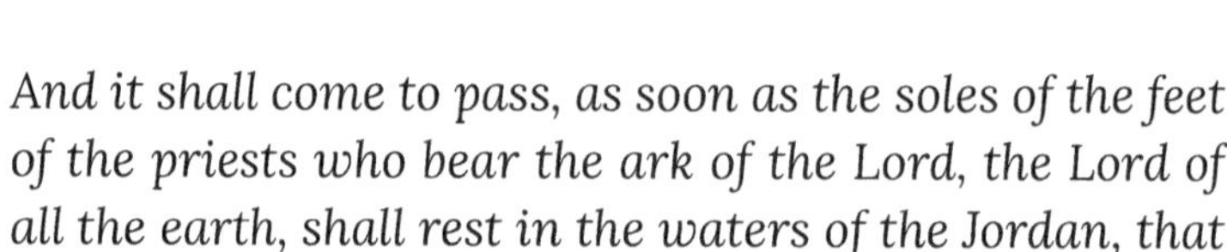

And it shall come to pass, as soon as the soles of the feet of the priests who bear the ark of the Lord, the Lord of all the earth, shall rest in the waters of the Jordan, that the waters of the Jordan shall be cut off, the waters that come down from upstream, and they shall stand as a heap.

— Joshua 3:13

Years later, Israel stood again at the Jordan, this time facing the Promised Land (Joshua 3:1).

The river was in flood stage. Violent. Loud. Totally impassable.

God didn't say, "Wait while I part it."

He didn't say, "Trust me from a safe distance."

He said, "Stand in it."

The priests had to step in first. The miracle waited for them (Joshua 3:15–16).

You don't get dry ground without wet feet. The river only parts after someone is willing to step in.

The Jordan is not incidental. It marks the place where trust becomes obedience—where belief gets wet.

———◦———

*He did not waver at the promise of God through unbelief,
but was strengthened in faith, giving glory to God.*
— Romans 4:20

Centuries before that, another man stood at an edge. Abraham heard a command that made even less sense:

"Leave your country" (Genesis 12:1).

He left.

"Offer Isaac" (Genesis 22:2).

He climbed.

Every defining moment of Abraham's life is marked not merely by what he believed, but by where he walked.

Paul tells us Abraham was justified by faith (Romans 4:3).

James tells us that faith was made visible in obedience (James 2:21–22).

Same tree.
Same faith.
Different angles.

Faith saves. But saving faith doesn't stay seated.

Abraham didn't freeze at the edge. He stepped where belief pointed.

———◦———

But without faith it is impossible to please Him, for he who comes to God must believe that He is, and that He is a rewarder of those who diligently seek Him.
— Hebrews 11:6

Let's be honest. We're usually pretty good at believing.

We admire the Bible.
We quote the promises.
We nod at the commands.

But a lot of the time, we believe the bridge exists while we're still standing on solid ground.

The writer of Hebrews lays it out plainly.

First: you must believe that He exists. Most people check that box. Second: you must believe that He rewards those who actually seek Him.

The second clause is the edge. The first one is just the parking lot.

It's one thing to believe that God is real. Even the demons believe—and tremble (James 2:19). Their doctrine may be technically correct, but they are still lost.

Hell is not lacking in orthodox believers; it is full of rebels who knew the truth and refused to obey it.

It's another thing entirely to believe He'll meet you while you're in motion.

Naaman believed God could heal. It became faith when he dipped the seventh time.

Israel believed God could part water. It became faith when their sandals broke the surface.

Abraham believed God could raise the dead. It became faith when he raised the knife.

The bridge doesn't show you how strong it is while you're studying the blueprints. It shows its strength when you're standing on it.

Every story of faith begins at the edge.

Edges aren't comfortable places. They demand a decision. And decisions demand movement.

The bridge will not come to you.

You must possess what you profess.

CHAPTER FIFTEEN

The Placebo

Why Feeling Better Isn't Getting Better

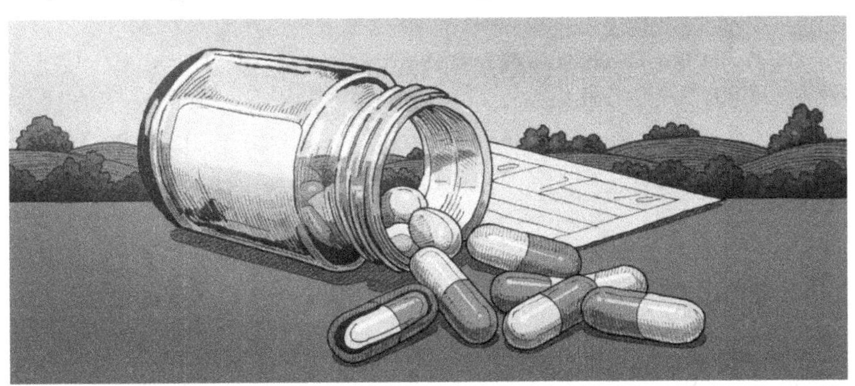

> *Not everyone who says to Me, "Lord, Lord," shall enter the king-dom of heaven, but he who does the will of My Father in heaven.*
> — Matthew 7:21

Back in 1996, the *New England Journal of Medicine* published a quiet little bomb.[1]

Doctors found that a sugar pill can act like real medicine. Just wrap it in enough authority with the white coat, the calm voice, and the confident tone. When you do, the body often reacts as if the drug is real. Pain drops. Endorphins kick in. Blood pressure starts behaving itself.

No actual drugs are required, only the appearance of medicine. The patient says they feel better, and technically they are not lying.

But the disease is still there. The placebo didn't cure anything. It only convinced the body to stop complaining. Relief without remission.

That word—remission—is both a medical term and a biblical one. It's what you say when the scans come back clean. The thing is gone. The record's wiped. The diagnosis is nowhere to be found. Placebos don't do that.

For the last century or so, modern Christianity has mastered the spiritual sugar pill.

It's neat. It's efficient. It's easy to hand out to a crowd. It fits perfectly on a tract and works wonders at the end of a sermon. The music swells. The lights soften. You start to feel like something big is about to happen.

It's called the "sinner's prayer."

You probably know the drill:

Say the words.
Admit the problem.
Invite Jesus into your heart.
Congratulations. You're saved.

There's just one problem.

You cannot find it anywhere in Scripture. Not in the Gospels, not in Acts, and not in the letters.

You'll find lots of people praying. Confession, repentance, tears, and desperation.

But you won't ever see an apostle telling a lost person, "Just bow your head and repeat after me."

That absence should bother us.

Because if the apostles never preached it, where did it come from? And if it's a placebo... then where's the cure?

Jesus compared salvation to a door (John 10:9).

Doors are funny things. Everybody loves them when they're open, but not so much when they're closed.

Noah knew that better than anyone. It was not enough to admire the vessel from outside. Rescue required entrance.

For laying aside the commandment of God, you hold the tradition of men—the washing of pitchers and cups, and many other such things you do. He said to them, "All too well you reject the commandment of God, that you may keep your tradition."

— Mark 7:8–9

Religion has always had a talent for creating traditions (Matthew 15:8–9). It's not always out of rebellion. Sometimes it's for the sake of convenience.

You start with a command. Then you make a little adjustment. Then another. Eventually, the adjustment replaces the command altogether.

The history of baptism shows this perfectly.

In the early church, baptism was a big, intentional deal. Adults heard the gospel, believed it, repented, and were immersed in water. It was public. It was decisive. And it was sometimes inconvenient.

Then history intervened.

By the fourth century, Christianity had changed. It went from a persecuted movement to the official religion of the empire. Suddenly, it was a good career move to be a Christian. It was politically useful and socially respectable.

Which created a logistical problem. Everyone needed to be "in."

Infant baptism solved that problem.

No messy conversions. No awkward adult decisions. Just sprinkle the baby, record the name, and another citizen of Christendom appears.

The church gained a roster. The empire stayed tidy. Everyone slept better.

Centuries later, revivalists walked into churches full of baptized members. Their hearts had never changed. They'd been sprinkled, but they'd never actually repented.

So the pendulum swung the other way. Since baptism could no longer serve as the moment of conversion, something else had to take its place.

Enter the prayer.

Simple. Emotional. Repeatable. Perfect for revival tents and altar calls.

And just like that, salvation quietly moved.

From covenant to confidence.
From obedience to experience.
From entering a door... to saying the right words.

—◦—

*If you confess with your mouth the Lord Jesus and be-
lieve in your heart that God has raised Him from the
dead, you will be saved.*
— Romans 10:9

Those who defend the sinner's prayer usually point to Romans 10.
Say the words. Believe the fact. Collect the prize.

But Romans 10:9 isn't the whole story.

Paul wasn't writing a script for an altar call, and you can't quote
him while trying to detour around Romans 6.

He was writing to baptized believers in Rome who had already
obeyed what he calls "that form of doctrine" (Romans 6:17).

The modern "Romans Road" is paved carefully to bypass the river.
But Paul's road runs straight through it: "We were buried with Him
through baptism into death" (Romans 6:4).

Buried.

Not admired.
Not symbolically acknowledged.

Buried.

That's a remarkable way to describe salvation if the entire event
happens in a single sentence.

Baptism is often reduced to "an outward sign of an inward reality."
But Paul's language is stronger than that. Grace is not merely
inward, and baptism is not merely outward.

In the Roman world, saying "Jesus is Lord" wasn't some quiet devotional phrase. It was a public pledge of allegiance that could cost you your family, your job, or even your life.

Paul wasn't describing a prayer. He was describing loyalty.

And now why are you waiting? Arise and be baptized, and wash away your sins, calling on the name of the Lord.

— Acts 22:16

Paul's own conversion proves the point. Luke tells the story three times in Acts. It may be the greatest baptismal drama of the New Testament.

On the road to Damascus, Paul met Jesus. He believed instantly. He was trembling. He called Him "Lord." He even fasted and prayed for three days straight.

If salvation by sincerity had a poster child, Paul was it.

But Luke does not present Paul as a saved man waiting around for a religious souvenir. Jesus did not bypass the message He had entrusted to His people. Even Paul had to come through the front door.

Which raises a question.

If Paul was already saved on that road, what exactly was Ananias doing three days later? Telling a saved man to wash away sins he no longer had?

That's not clarification. That's contradiction.

When Ananias shows up, he doesn't say, "Well, you've already prayed, so you're good to go."

He says, "And now why are you waiting? Arise and be baptized, and wash away your sins, calling on the name of the Lord."

Look at the order.

Three days of prayer. Sin still present. Baptism still commanded. Washing still future.

The order is stubborn. Ananias does not place washing before baptism, as though baptism merely pictured cleansing already received. He places baptism *with* the washing.

And that matters, because baptism is not presented as a righteous deed we perform to impress God. Paul himself would later say God saves us "not by works of righteousness which we have done," but "according to His mercy," through "the washing of regeneration and renewing of the Holy Spirit" (Titus 3:5).

Baptism is where God does what we cannot do.[2]

Regenerate.
Renew.
Save by mercy.

The call wasn't a whispered prayer from dry ground. It was an appeal made through the water.

Baptism is the sinner's prayer without syllables. The body says what the mouth has been trying to say all along:

"Lord, I surrender."

———◄O►———

Now as they went down the road, they came to some water. And the eunuch said, "See, here is water. What hinders me from being baptized?" So he commanded the chariot to stand still. And both Philip and the eunuch went down into the water, and he baptized him.
— Acts 8:36–38

Acts 8 gives us another snapshot.

Philip preached Jesus to the Ethiopian eunuch. We don't have the transcript. We don't know if Philip preached for five minutes or five hours. But we know exactly how it landed.

The moment water appeared, the eunuch knew what question came next: "See, here is water. What hinders me from being baptized?"

He didn't ask what prayer to repeat.
He didn't ask whether baptism could wait.
He didn't ask for a private spiritual moment in the chariot.

Philip didn't sprinkle him from a travel jug.

Philip preached Jesus. The Ethiopian looked for water.

That reaction tells us everything. In the first century, preaching Jesus apparently included preaching the place where a person enters Him.

They stopped. They went down into the water. They got wet.

Because in the first century, everyone understood something we've managed to complicate:

Water is where you meet the Lord.

Not by works of righteousness which we have done, but according to His mercy He saved us, through the washing of regeneration and renewing of the Holy Spirit.
— Titus 3:5

At this point someone usually objects. "Isn't baptism a work?" That's a fair question.

Imagine a wealthy man offers you a hundred-dollar bill. It's a gift. You did nothing to earn it. But instead of handing it to you, he throws it into a pond.

"It's yours," he says. "Go get it."

You step in. You get wet. You retrieve the bill.

Did you earn the money?

Of course not.

You went to where the gift was placed.

Baptism isn't wages. It's where the gift is received.

Water doesn't create salvation. Jesus does. But water is where He put the promise.

You cannot receive a gift you refuse to pick up.

—◆O◆—

Let us draw near with a true heart in full assurance of faith, having our hearts sprinkled from an evil conscience and our bodies washed with pure water.
— Hebrews 10:22

There is another cruel part about placebo religion. It manufactures the doubt it claims to cure.

If salvation depends on whether you said the right words with the right amount of sincerity, then you'll never be certain.

Did I mean it enough? Did I say it right? Maybe I should pray it again. Just in case.

Children repeat the prayer. Teenagers recite it at youth rallies. Adults whisper it in hospital rooms when the machines start beeping louder.

Because if salvation is merely a sentence, you had better pronounce it perfectly.

But covenant events leave memories. You remember the day. The place. The water.

It's hard to doubt something that once left you dripping wet.

—————◄O►—————

*And there are three that bear witness on earth: the
Spirit, the water, and the blood; and these three agree
as one.*

— 1 John 5:8

John presents a courtroom scene with three witnesses (Deuteronomy 19:15).

Spirit.
Water.
Blood.

Peter uses similar legal language when he says baptism is an appeal to God for a good conscience (1 Peter 3:21).

An appeal is something you make to a judge. The verdict is remission. Not a feeling. A release. The disease is gone.

A placebo manages your symptoms. Remission removes the problem.

Isaiah described it vividly: scarlet becomes snow (Isaiah 1:18). Scarlet dye didn't rinse away. Once it bonded to fabric, it was there for good.

But God promised something stronger.

To remove that kind of stain, you need a solvent. God places that solvent in the water. Not because the water itself cleanses you, but because that's where the sinner meets the blood of Jesus.

And that's where the Spirit is given.

The water isn't the seal. The Spirit is. You don't mark yourself. He does.

Baptism is the place of the encounter (Acts 2:38). The Spirit is the mark of ownership (Ephesians 1:13; 4:30). That's where the seal is pressed.

Three witnesses.

Spirit.
Water.
Blood.

One testimony.

Who formerly were disobedient, when once the Divine longsuffering waited in the days of Noah, while the ark was being prepared, in which a few, that is, eight souls, were saved through water. There is also an antitype which now saves us—baptism (not the removal of the filth of the flesh, but the answer of a good conscience toward God), through the resurrection of Jesus Christ.

— 1 Peter 3:20–21

Peter ties the whole thing back to Noah. Eight people saved through water. The same water that destroyed the world carried the ark.

Outside the Ark: judgment.
Inside the Ark: salvation.

Same water.
Different outcome.

One group was saved. The other only felt safe.

The sinner's prayer admires the Ark.

Baptism boards it.

For God so loved the world that He gave His only begotten Son, that whoever believes in Him should not perish but have everlasting life.

— John 3:16

John 3:16 is the most famous verse in the Bible for a reason.

But it isn't a loophole. It's the headline.

Belief opens the door to life. But in Scripture, belief never sits still. It moves. Obeys. Takes a step.

God didn't ask us to recite our trust; He asked us to show it.

Salvation isn't a magical phrase. It's a covenant.

Covenants aren't sealed in whispers; they're sealed in blood. Scripture points to the water as the place where that blood meets a life. That's where the door has always been.

A placebo can manage the symptoms until the disease finishes its work. It can calm the patient right up to the moment the door closes.

But the Flood will not ask whether you felt saved.

It will ask whether you were onboard.

CHAPTER SIXTEEN

The Probate

When the Decision Is No Longer Yours

> *There is a way that seems right to a man, but its end is the way of death.*
>
> — Proverbs 14:12

Back in 1995, a man named McArthur Wheeler walked into two Pittsburgh banks and robbed them in broad daylight.[1]

Instead of a mask, he covered his face in lemon juice. He was convinced it would make him invisible to surveillance cameras. His confidence rested on bad science. Since lemon juice can be used as invisible ink, he figured it'd also hide his face if liberally applied. Wheeler even smiled for the cameras before he left. He was certain his disguise was foolproof.

Surveillance footage was shown on the news. Tips poured in. Within hours, the police arrested him. When they asked why he used lemon juice, he said, "I thought it'd make me invisible." He even claimed to have successfully tested the theory with his

Polaroid camera. Investigators later concluded the test failed because of a broken camera or operator error.

The "lemon juice bandit" tells us something uncomfortable: we often trust ideas that feel safe rather than ideas that are true.

Confidence built on ignorance is only ignorance wearing a grin.

And nowhere is this more dangerous than in theology.

Then he said to Jesus, "Lord, remember me when You come into Your kingdom." And Jesus said to him, "Assuredly, I say to you, today you will be with Me in Paradise."

— Luke 23:42–43

Three crosses stood on a hill that looked like a skull. One man, labeled "King of the Jews," bore the weight of every sin. The other two were criminals, bleeding out beside Him. Around them, soldiers gambled for His clothes, priests jeered, and the crowd heckled. Matthew adds that the men crucified with Him did the same.

Then something shifted.

Somewhere between the taunts and the labored breaths, one of the thieves became quiet. Maybe it was the silence of a Man who refused to save Himself.

Whatever turned in him, it left him with nothing to bargain with. No record to appeal to. No future obedience to promise. No time to make restitution.

Only breath.

And he spent it on the one request no dying criminal should have had the courage to make.

He turned to his partner in crime. "Don't you fear God? We're getting what we deserve. But this Man has done nothing wrong."

Then came the line that cracked open eternity: "Jesus, remember me when You come into Your kingdom."

Jesus—still bleeding, barely breathing—replied, "Today, you will be with Me in Paradise."

By morning, condemned.
By noon, forgiven.

By nightfall, home.

Be diligent to present yourself approved to God, a worker who does not need to be ashamed, rightly dividing the word of truth.

— 2 Timothy 2:15

The thief on the cross might be the most famous criminal in history. He's also history's most celebrated deathbed conversion.

His life showed no record of devotion or charity. He wasn't a prophet or a priest, just a criminal with bad timing and a flicker of faith. By almost any measure, his life was a total failure—until his final few minutes.

Strange, isn't it, that a man whose name we don't know has become a regular guest in Sunday sermons? He's the poster child for "deathbed conversions" and a theological chess piece in one of Christianity's oldest debates: Do you need to be baptized to be saved?

Ask that question, and sooner or later, someone will bring up the thief on the cross. The argument usually sounds like this: "He believed, and that was good enough for me."

It sounds airtight—until you start asking questions.

For where there is a testament, there must also of necessity be the death of the testator. For a testament is in force after men are dead, since it has no power at all while the testator lives. Therefore not even the first covenant was dedicated without blood.

— Hebrews 9:16–18

People love shortcuts. But shortcuts have a way of missing the mark.

In contract law, timing determines everything. To understand the thief, you don't need a degree in theology. You need to understand the mechanics of a will.

Jesus has the power and authority to save anyone He chooses. While on earth, He could look a person in the eye and pronounce forgiveness, salvation, or mercy: the paralyzed man (Luke 5:20), Zacchaeus (Luke 19:9), the woman caught in adultery (John 8:11), and the thief (Luke 23:43).

But after His death, the legal framework changed.

When someone says, "The thief wasn't baptized," the text doesn't say. One thing we do know for sure: the thief wasn't a Christian. In fact, at that moment, no one was.

Different era.
Different covenant.
Different rules.

The thief died under the Old Covenant. The Cross hadn't completed its work, the curtain hadn't torn (Matthew 27:51), and the tomb wasn't yet empty. He never heard Peter's sermon at Pentecost (Acts 2) or Jesus' command, "He who believes and is baptized will be saved; but he who does not believe will be condemned" (Mark 16:16).

Before the crucifixion, there was no body to be baptized into (Romans 6:4; 1 Corinthians 12:13). Baptism into Christ had not been commanded yet because Jesus had not died.

That's why the thief's story, however beautiful, can't be our pattern for salvation. He was the last man saved before the will was read. His story was mercy at the finish line. Ours is mercy at the starting gun.

A will does not run on sentiment. It may be full of love. It may name heirs. It may promise an inheritance large enough to change a family forever. But until the death occurs, the document is not handing out anything. The beneficiaries may be known. The promises may be written. The intentions may be clear.

But the estate has not settled.

Nobody walks into probate court before the funeral and says, "I know what the will says, so I'll take my inheritance now." That is not how wills work. Timing matters. Authority matters. Death matters.

That is exactly the point Hebrews makes. The death of the testator does not merely prove the will was serious. It puts the will into force. Before death, the testator can speak directly. After death, the testament governs.

That distinction matters at Calvary.

The thief did not live long enough to hear the risen Christ commission His apostles. He did not stand in Jerusalem when Peter preached the first gospel sermon after the Resurrection. He did not hear Peter answer the crowd after they were cut to the heart and asked what they should do.

He died before the announcement.

Before Pentecost, Jesus could personally pardon a man standing in front of Him. Or hanging beside Him. He could forgive sins on earth because He had authority on earth to forgive sins. But after His death, burial, resurrection, and ascension, that mercy was published.

That is what Acts 2 is. Not a committee decision. Not a church tradition that drifted in later. Not fine print added by overzealous apostles.

Pentecost is the public reading of the will.

The King had died. The King had risen. The King had taken His seat. And now the terms of entrance into His kingdom were announced in the open, by His apostles, under the authority of His Spirit.

That is why the thief cannot be used as a loophole. He belongs to the last page of one covenant, not the first page of ours.

The thief received mercy before the will was read.

We answer to the King after it.

Though it is only a man's covenant, yet if it is confirmed, no one annuls or adds to it.

— Galatians 3:15

When we lean on the thief as an argument against baptism, we turn him into lemon juice for theology—something that feels protective but isn't. It creates false confidence. Like citrus on the skin, it doesn't shield us from judgment; it leaves us exposed.

Saving faith isn't built on exceptions. It's built on covenant.

Jesus forgave sins while He walked the earth—the paralytic, the adulterous woman, the thief. But after His death, the testament was in force.

The question isn't, *Can I be saved like the thief?*

It's, *Will I be saved like the people who heard the gospel after the Cross?*

No one in Acts appealed to the thief for a loophole.

At Pentecost, they were told to repent and be baptized, and they obeyed. Saul was told to arise and be baptized, and he obeyed (Acts 22:16). The jailer was told what to do, and he obeyed that very night (Acts 16:30–33).

They didn't argue. They obeyed.

The thief was promised paradise. We are promised adoption.

The thief is an exception.

And exceptions don't define the rule.

Go therefore and make disciples of all the nations, baptizing them in the name of the Father and of the Son and of the Holy Spirit.

— Matthew 28:19

The Great Commission is the constitution of the new kingdom.

It was given after the Resurrection, under the authority of a risen King, to a world on this side of the Cross.

We are not standing at Calvary hoping for a private pardon. We are standing at Pentecost, hearing the public reading of His will.

And the will does not leave baptism buried in the fine print. In Matthew 28:19–20, Jesus puts baptism at the front door of disciple-making: go, make disciples, baptize, teach. That order matters. Baptism is not one more chore for people already inside the kingdom. It is part of how they cross the threshold and board the Ark.

Repent.
Be baptized.
Begin again.

The thief trusted a dying Savior.

We obey a risen King.

No amount of theological lemon juice will make a command disappear.

CHAPTER SEVENTEEN

The Burial Plot

What Has to Die First

> *Or do you not know that as many of us as were baptized into Christ Jesus were baptized into His death?*
>
> — Romans 6:3

Here's a strange detail from Roman law. You could be erased without spilling your blood.

This terrifying concept was called *capitis deminutio*.[1] Literally, it means "a decrease of a head."

Your citizenship was revoked, your family severed, and your property confiscated. Biologically speaking, you were still breathing. But legally, you no longer existed.

This is a difficult concept for us to grasp because we think identity is internal. *I think, therefore, I am.*

Rome thought differently. You were who the law said you were. And if the law declares you dead, you were dead.

Paul knew that system well because he was a card-carrying Roman citizen. When he explained salvation to the church in Rome, he didn't use poetic language. He used the language of execution.

His argument was shocking: to be saved, you need more than forgiveness. Sin pays wages, and the wages are death (Romans 6:23). Either you die with your sins, or you die with Jesus.

You need a death certificate.

Therefore we were buried with Him through baptism into death, that just as Christ was raised from the dead by the glory of the Father, even so we also should walk in newness of life.

— Romans 6:4

In the Epistles, the water metaphor sharpens. Baptism becomes a grave. Paul doesn't say we believed into His death. He doesn't say we repented into His death. He says we were baptized into His death.

If the death and burial happened before baptism, Paul chose a strange place to put the grave. And if salvation happens before baptism, then Paul is burying someone already alive.

You can't polish a corpse into a saint. You don't renovate the old life; you crucify it (Romans 6:6). Then you bury it—not by sprinkling dirt on it, but by putting it six feet under.

If baptism is merely a public profession, a nice religious gesture, then yes, it is a work.

But if baptism is a burial?

The dead don't perform.
The dead don't work.
The dead are acted upon.

When a body is lowered into the ground, it doesn't assist the gravedigger. It doesn't help shovel the dirt. It doesn't contribute. It lies there.

In baptism, you're not the worker. You're the corpse. Not the hero. The body.

Salvation is not you doing something impressive for God. It's God doing something final to you.

In Him you were also circumcised with the circumcision made without hands, by putting off the body of the sins of the flesh, by the circumcision of Christ, buried with Him in baptism, in which you also were raised with Him through faith in the working of God, who raised Him from the dead.

— Colossians 2:11–12

For centuries, Christians have argued that we're saved by grace through faith (Ephesians 2:8–9). They're correct. We can't earn it. We can't work for it.

Because of that truth, many grow nervous around baptism. It involves water. It involves movement. It looks physical. It looks like something a human does. So they reduce it to symbolism.

Paul anticipates that objection. He compares baptism to circumcision, but with a twist: this is a circumcision made *without human hands*.

Yes, human hands lower a person into water. But Paul insists that the real operation is performed by God.

Think of surgery.

If you have a tumor, you go to the hospital. You lie on the table. You submit to anesthesia. You do nothing. The surgeon cuts, removes, repairs. When you wake up, you don't boast about the "work" you did.

You submitted.

Faith is the decision to get on the table. Baptism is the surgery. God is the Surgeon.

Paul says we are raised in baptism *"through faith in the working of God"* (Colossians 2:12). That phrase matters. Baptism is not faith in water, wet clothes, or human choreography. It is faith in the God who promises to work there. We submit. We call on His name. God does the cutting, burying, and raising.

To call baptism a "work" is to confuse the patient with the Doctor.

You don't brag about how well you lay still on the table.

> *For by one Spirit we were all baptized into one body—whether Jews or Greeks, whether slaves or free—and have all been made to drink into one Spirit.*
> — 1 Corinthians 12:13

There is a tiny word in the Greek that carries more weight than it looks like it should: *into*. The word implies movement.

"Baptized *into* Jesus."
"Baptized *into* His death."
"Baptized *into* one body."

The pattern is hard to miss. Not near one body. Not around one body. Into one body. Baptism is not presented as a ceremony for people already safely inside. It is the crossing *into* the body of Christ.

That matters because "body" is not decoration in Paul's theology. It is identity. It is belonging. It is where the old divisions lose their authority. Jew or Greek. Slave or free. Whatever named you before, something greater names you now.

Scripture never describes someone as being "prayed *into* Jesus." It describes them as being baptized *into* Him.

Into is a threshold word.
Two jurisdictions.
One crossing.

Not because you're already *in*.
Because you are outside.
And then you are *in*.

The water itself isn't magical.

It is the moment of transfer.

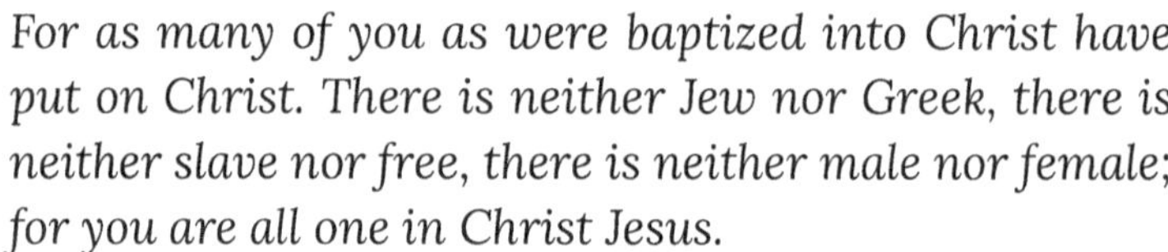

For as many of you as were baptized into Christ have put on Christ. There is neither Jew nor Greek, there is neither slave nor free, there is neither male nor female; for you are all one in Christ Jesus.

— Galatians 3:27–28

Clothing matters.

In Rome, when a boy came of age, they stripped away the garment of childhood and put on the toga of adulthood. It wasn't just a wardrobe change; it was a legal transformation. It was the moment the law began to recognize him as a man.[2]

Paul borrows that imagery. Baptism is a wardrobe change backed by the authority of heaven. The old rags are stripped. Jesus is put on. Not symbolically. Legally.

Galatians 3:27 does not say, "As many of you as had already put on Christ were later baptized." It says, "*For as many of you as were baptized into Christ have put on Christ.*"

Baptism is not treated as a symbol that follows the clothing. It is where the clothing happens.

God has always been the One who covers shame.

In the parable of the wedding banquet, the Master provides the clothes (Matthew 22:11–13; Isaiah 61:10). In the King's hall, you don't wear your own attire. To stand there in your own rags isn't just an eyesore; it's an insult to the Host. It's a rebellion against His provision. If the King hands you a robe, you put it on, or you are cast into the outer darkness.

When a person rises from the water, God doesn't see a rehabilitated version of their old self. He sees His Son. That person has undergone *capitis deminutio*. Their former legal status is erased (1 Corinthians 6:11).

The ledger is cleared.
The charges collapse.
The case is dismissed.

You aren't a defendant anymore. You're a guest at the King's table, wearing His clothes, not your own.

> *For if we have been united together in the likeness of His death, certainly we also shall be in the likeness of His resurrection.*
>
> — Romans 6:5

Everyone wants resurrection, but nobody wants the burial dirt under their fingernails.

We try to add Jesus to our lives like an accessory. A moral upgrade. A spiritual supplement. But God isn't interested in improving the old you. He is interested in making you new.

Resurrection requires a corpse; you can't resurrect what hasn't first died.

In Romans 6, Paul doesn't even bother arguing for baptism; he simply asks, "Do you not know...?" He assumes the burial has already happened. He isn't giving a suggestion; he's stating a fact.

Paul's argument depends on baptism being something the Roman Christians could look back to as the decisive break with the old life. He does not tell them to search their feelings, replay a private prayer, or locate the exact moment they first believed. He points them to their baptism and says, in effect, "Remember where the old you was buried."

Paul continues: How can we who died to sin live in it any longer? If the old self was drowned, why are you trying to revive it?

Baptism isn't a graduation ceremony; it's the starting block. You don't cross the starting line of a race and sit down. You cross and start running.

The grave isn't the end of the story. It's the only way to begin.

Even when we were dead in trespasses, made us alive together with Christ (by grace you have been saved).
— Ephesians 2:5

Salvation isn't self-improvement. It's God declaring your old life beyond repair. It's execution followed by resurrection.

The old you isn't cleaned up. It's buried.

The new you isn't self-made. It's raised (2 Corinthians 5:17).

In Roman law, civil death stripped you of everything. In Jesus, death grants you everything. A new name, a new status, a new family.

The law that once condemned you now recognizes a different person (Romans 8:1).

The grave isn't a threat. It's mercy. And if you want resurrection life, there's only one way to get it.

You cannot skip the grave.

You must go through the burial plot.

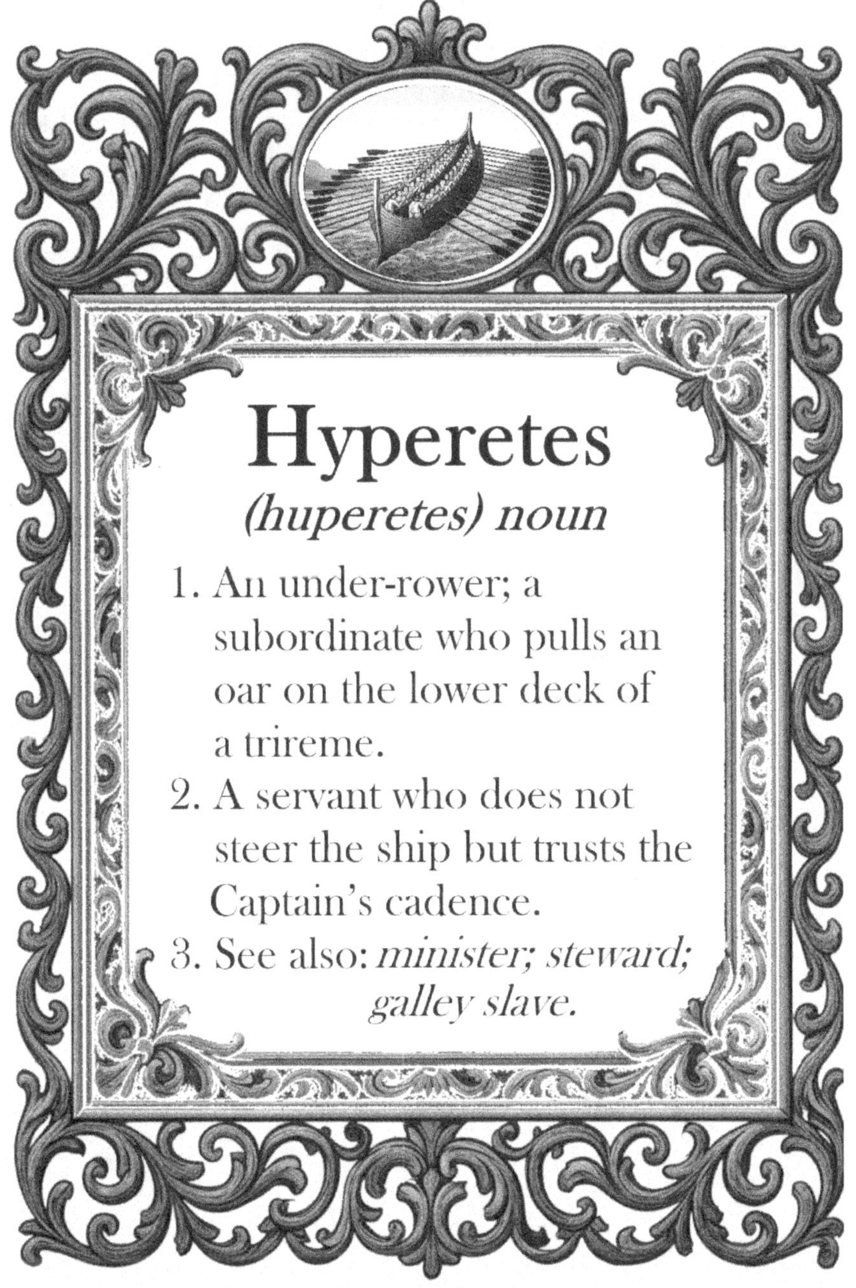

Hyperetes

(huperetes) noun

1. An under-rower; a subordinate who pulls an oar on the lower deck of a trireme.
2. A servant who does not steer the ship but trusts the Captain's cadence.
3. See also: *minister; steward; galley slave.*

Chapter Eighteen

The Glass Cage

Safe, Stable... and Stuck

> *And they continued steadfastly in the apostles' doctrine and fellowship, in the breaking of bread, and in prayers.*
>
> — Acts 2:42

In September 1991, eight people stepped through an airlock into a brand-new world. They were deep in the Arizona desert, dressed in matching red jumpsuits.

They were entering Biosphere 2, a three-acre glass ecosystem. Think of it as a tiny earth-in-a-bottle. It had everything: a rainforest, a mangrove swamp, a savannah, and even a toy-sized ocean.

The idea was simple. Seal the doors. Balance the system. Prove that humans could build a perfect world. Nothing would come in. Nothing would go out. Just eight humans living on their own private planet.

The crew was optimistic. They waved to the cameras. The airlock hissed shut. The experiment began.

It took less than a year for the "perfect world" to turn on them.[1]

Oxygen levels started dropping—slowly, quietly, as if someone were turning down the volume on the atmosphere. Simple chores left them gasping for air. Soon, sleep apnea became the norm.

To make matters worse, the pollinating insects died off. Crops struggled to grow. Ants and cockroaches, sensing a power vacuum, stepped up to claim their new empire.

But the real collapse? It wasn't biological.

It was human.

Trapped inside the glass cage, the biospherians split into rival factions. They stopped speaking to each other. They hoarded food. They sabotaged each other's experiments.

A team of world-class scientists slowly turned into warring tribes.

By the time the airlock finally opened two years later, the ecosystem was failing. But the relationships inside? Toxic enough to qualify for reality television.

The engineers had built something brilliant.

But they forgot to account for the people they put inside it.

Now I plead with you, brethren, by the name of our Lord Jesus Christ, that you all speak the same thing, and that there be no divisions among you, but that you be perfectly joined together in the same mind and in the same judgment.

— 1 Corinthians 1:10

To understand why the church survives where Biosphere failed, look at the Greek word Paul uses to describe himself.

The word is *hyperetes* (1 Corinthians 4:1).[2]

Modern Bibles translate it politely as "servant" or "minister." But a first-century reader would've smelled the sweat in that word immediately. Because a *hyperetes* carried the image of an under-rower.

In the ancient world, massive warships called *triremes* ruled the sea. They were powered by three tiers of oars. Deep in the belly of the ship, you'd find the rowers.

They sat in the dark. They pulled heavy oars. They couldn't see the ocean. They couldn't see the battle. And they definitely couldn't steer the ship.

All they could do was listen to the rhythm of the drum and row in sync with the person beside them.

If one rower pulled at the wrong speed or in the wrong direction, the oars would crash together. The whole ship would stall.

Unity wasn't inspirational. It was *mechanical.*

When Paul calls himself a *hyperetes*, he is making something very clear:

He wasn't the captain.

He was pulling an oar.

The church was never designed to be a room full of captains arguing over who gets the wheel. It was designed to be a galley.

That was Corinth's problem. They were turning under-rowers into banners. "I am of Paul." "I am of Apollos." "I am of Cephas." Same ship. Different flags.

When Paul says Christ did not send him "to baptize, but to preach the gospel" (1 Corinthians 1:17), he is not minimizing baptism. He is refusing to let the baptizer become the brand.

Unity isn't about everyone agreeing on every preference. It's about everyone rowing the same stroke (Ephesians 4:4–6).

You can't have a mutiny if everyone's too busy rowing.

Let a man so consider us, as servants of Christ and stewards of the mysteries of God.
— 1 Corinthians 4:1

That raises a question.

We don't naturally behave this way. Put a group of strangers in a closed system—like the one in the desert—and hierarchies appear immediately. Status games. Power struggles. Everyone has an opinion on how to steer the ship.

So why didn't the early church implode the way Biosphere did?

Because the entry requirement destroys the hierarchy.

Picture two men standing at the edge of a baptismal pool.

One is a Navy SEAL. A product of one of the most brutal training programs on earth. Disciplined, capable, and respected.

Next to him stands a convicted criminal. A man who spent decades making one bad decision after another.

To the rest of the world, these men live on totally different planets. One's celebrated; the other's avoided.

But something strange happens at the water's edge: their resumes suddenly become useless.

The soldier must admit that his strength can't save him. The criminal must admit that his record can't condemn him. Then both of them go under the same water (Romans 6:3–4).

The medals disappear.
The criminal record disappears.

And when they come back up, they aren't a hero and a failure anymore.

They're brothers.

Baptism does something radical. It erases status.

Inside the Ark, there aren't any elite passengers (James 2:1–4).

There are only the rescued.

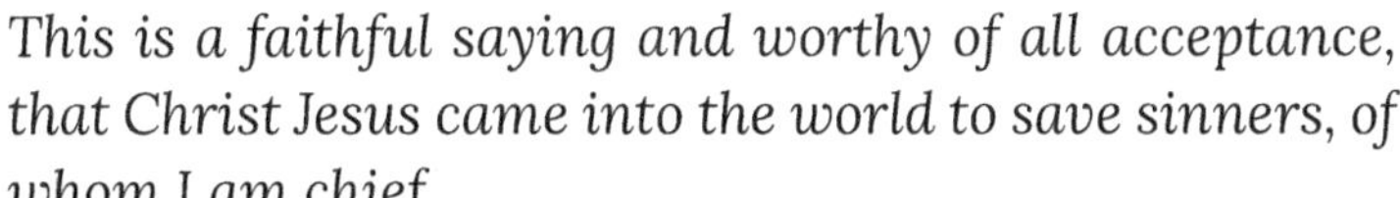

This is a faithful saying and worthy of all acceptance, that Christ Jesus came into the world to save sinners, of whom I am chief.

— 1 Timothy 1:15

Now that sounds noble when we're talking about "normal" sinners. But the idea gets a lot more uncomfortable when the sinner isn't exactly average.

On May 10, 1994, a minister walked into a prison in Wisconsin. Waiting for him was a man standing beside a stainless-steel whirlpool tub.

The prisoner was Jeffrey Dahmer.[3]

Dahmer had raped, murdered, and dismembered 17 young men and boys. His crimes horrified the world.

They were sons, brothers, and friends, and their families carried wounds no sentence in a book can measure.

Society didn't just want him punished. It wanted him erased.

Then, inside his prison cell, something unexpected happened. Dahmer began studying the Bible. He read the command to repent and be baptized. Then he asked for the water.

The minister didn't ask him to undo the impossible. He asked for his confession.

Dahmer stepped into the tub. The minister lowered him into the water.

When Dahmer came up, the minister said something that absolutely outraged people.

"Welcome to the family of God."

The backlash was instant. People lost their minds. Letters poured in saying things like, "If Jeffrey Dahmer's in heaven, I don't want to be there."

That reaction reveals something uncomfortable about us.

We *love* grace when it saves "respectable" sinners.

We *hate* grace when it saves monsters.

But the Ark was never designed for the clean. It was built for the unclean (Mark 2:17).

If the blood of Jesus is *strong* enough for a Sunday school teacher but too *weak* for Jeffrey Dahmer, we have a problem. Because if it can't save him, it isn't powerful enough to save us.

The water is the great leveler.

It washes away medals.

It washes away monsters.

Inside the Ark, we're all wet sinners who owe everything to the Captain.

But God demonstrates His own love toward us, in that while we were still sinners, Christ died for us.
— Romans 5:8

This is why the early church in Acts is so remarkable.

After Pentecost, thousands of people from different cultures found themselves inside the same spiritual vessel.

Parthians. Medes. Elamites. Romans. Jews. Proselytes. Different languages. Different customs. Different backgrounds.

By every sociological rule, the movement should have exploded in a week. Instead, Luke records something astonishing:

"They continued steadfastly in the apostles' doctrine and fellowship, in the breaking of bread, and in prayers" (Acts 2:42).

They didn't organize around personalities. They organized around doctrine.

That's a word that makes people a little twitchy these days. We prefer softer words like "community" or "journey." Doctrine sounds rigid.

But in a closed system, rigidity isn't cruelty. It's oxygen.

Doctrine is the air filtration system. Without it, the oxygen disappears and the system suffocates.

The early church didn't stay united because everyone liked the same things or voted the same way. They stayed united because they submitted to the same pattern (Romans 6:17).

They rowed to the same cadence.

> *Hold fast the pattern of sound words which you have heard from me, in faith and love which are in Christ Jesus.*
>
> — 2 Timothy 1:13

Every closed system tests the same instinct: when the air gets thin, who jumps?

Paul saw it on a ship bound for Rome. A massive storm had hit, and for 14 days the crew hadn't seen the sun or stars.

Eventually, the sailors tried to escape. They secretly lowered a lifeboat, pretending they were setting anchors. In reality, they were planning to abandon ship.

But Paul gave the centurion a blunt warning:

"Unless these men stay in the ship, you cannot be saved" (Acts 27:31).

The soldiers didn't hesitate. They cut the ropes. The lifeboat dropped into the sea and drifted away.

Which brings us to the hardest lesson of the Ark.

When things get messy, our first instinct is to lower a lifeboat. We want to bail when personalities clash, leadership fails, or storms begin to rage.

We start looking for a *better* church. A *purer* church. Maybe even no church at all.

But the protocol hasn't changed. Safety isn't found in the lifeboat you build yourself.

It's found in the ship *God* designed.

CHAPTER NINETEEN

The Ten Percent

Why Most People Are Still Wrong

> *Then one said to Him, "Lord, are there few who are saved?" And He said to them, "Strive to enter through the narrow gate, for many, I say to you, will seek to enter and will not be able."*
>
> — Luke 13:23-24

Scientists at Rensselaer Polytechnic Institute ran computer simulations to study how beliefs spread. They discovered something surprising.

If a belief is held by less than 10 percent of the population, it seldom spreads. It remains background noise.

But the moment it reaches 10 percent, it spreads fast. The shift isn't gradual. It's sudden. As long as those people are unwavering and committed, the idea takes off.

Suddenly the minority isn't weird.

It's contagious.

The majority doesn't get convinced so much as it tilts.

Researchers called it the 10% Rule.[1]

The idea is simple.

Most people are flexible. They compromise. They drift with the cultural current. But a small group that refuses to move eventually shifts the current itself.

This discovery surprised sociologists.

It shouldn't surprise anyone who has read the Bible.

God has always worked through minorities. Actually, He works with far less than 10 percent.

...eight souls were saved through water.
— 1 Peter 3:20

How many people died in the Flood?

Estimates of the world's population vary wildly. Some scholars suggest millions. Others imagine far more. Let's say there were 10 million people.

Noah's group only had eight.

Not eight thousand.
Not eight percent.

Eight.

That's 0.00008% of the population.

By every statistical model, Noah and his family were irrelevant. A rounding error. A tiny speck in the data.

And yet, when the floodwaters receded, that 0.00008% was 100% of the future.

Then the Lord said to Noah, "Come into the ark, you and all your household, because I have seen that you are righteous before Me in this generation."
— Genesis 7:1

Noah dealt with the pressure of the crowd for 120 years. He didn't just disagree with the majority. He disagreed with *everyone.*

No one told him he was right. No one applauded his obedience.

Human beings are herd creatures. We like to think we make up our own minds, but most of us are reading the room.

If enough people laugh at something, it starts to feel ridiculous. If enough people accept something, it starts to feel obvious. The crowd doesn't need an argument. It only needs volume.

Noah's miracle wasn't the boat; it's his refusal to quit. Building something strange is one thing. Building it while everyone is watching, laughing, and shrugging—that's something else.

God preserved humanity through a man who chose one voice over the noise of millions.

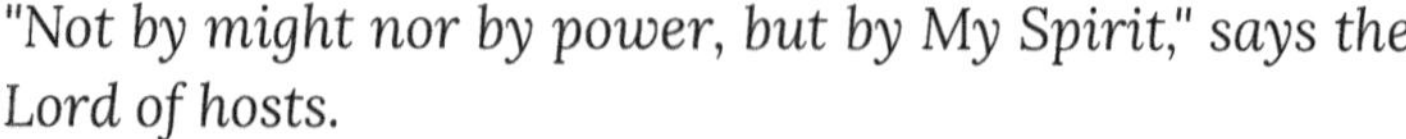

You shall not follow a crowd to do evil; nor shall you testify in a dispute so as to turn aside after many to pervert justice.

— Exodus 23:2

There's another layer to this.

The crowd doesn't just disagree. It normalizes.

Laugh at something long enough, and it'll stop feeling serious. Ignore something long enough, and it won't feel urgent anymore.

That's how truth erodes. Not by logic but by atmosphere. And the atmosphere is set by the crowd.

It doesn't feel like pressure. It feels like... everyone.

Noah was standing against a world that had learned to feel nothing about where it was going.

And that might be the hardest kind of resistance there is.

"Not by might nor by power, but by My Spirit," says the Lord of hosts.

— Zechariah 4:6

Noah isn't unique.

Gideon started with an army of 32,000 soldiers. God cut that number down to 300 (Judges 7:2–7). Less than one percent.

Why?

Because God doesn't need a crowd. He needs obedience that doesn't flinch.

Jesus did the same thing. He didn't assemble a panel of experts or recruit from the top schools. He picked twelve ordinary men from a place most people ignored (Mark 3:13–19). One of them would betray Him, which isn't exactly an ideal team-building strategy.

And yet with that fragile minority, He tipped the course of human history.

The New Testament church is described using the same language.

A remnant.
A little flock.
The salt of the earth.

Salt works precisely because it's used sparingly. A pinch changes the flavor of a whole meal.

But the salt must remain salty. The moment it tries to blend in, it disappears (Matthew 5:13).

The temptation to blend in haunts modern Christianity.

We assume that to change the culture we must resemble it. We smooth things out. We tone things down. We make everything a bit more agreeable.

It sounds nice.

But it doesn't work.

The majority has never been the measure of truth.

Influence doesn't come from blending in.

A compromised minority changes *nothing*.

A committed minority changes *everything*.

Noah didn't save the world by becoming more like it. He did the opposite. He built exactly what God told him to build (Genesis 6:22).

For 120 years he ignored the math. He ignored the culture. He ignored the mockery.

He kept building.

Until it started to rain.

> *For do I now persuade men, or God? Or do I seek to please men? For if I still pleased men, I would not be a bondservant of Christ.*
>
> — Galatians 1:10

We don't just notice crowds. We tend to follow them. There's a reason for that.

For most of human history, being wrong by yourself was dangerous. If the group ran, you ran. If the group stayed, you stayed.

Survival was social. It kept us alive. But now, it keeps us comfortable.

We look to the crowd for validation.

If enough people believe something, it *must* be right.

If enough people reject something, it *must* be wrong.

We don't say it out loud. But we feel it.

You see it when someone hesitates before speaking up. When a room leans one way, and the lone dissenter goes quiet. When a person knows the truth but checks the temperature first.

Consensus has gravity. Most people won't fight it. Standing against it feels reckless.

That's why Noah's story is so hard to process. Not because of the Flood. Because of the silence.

No support.
No confirmation.
No one saying, "You're on the right track."

Just one voice from God... against the whole world.

We like to imagine we would have stood with Noah.

But most people didn't.

Human nature hasn't changed.

Truth rarely travels with the majority.

But God has chosen the foolish things of the world to put to shame the wise, and God has chosen the weak things of the world to put to shame the things which are mighty.

— 1 Corinthians 1:27

The math never made sense. Eight people against the world. Three hundred against an army. Twelve against an empire.

And yet, that's how God works. Not through crowds, but through conviction.

We keep asking the wrong question.

"If this is true, why isn't everyone doing it?"

The better question is this:

"If everyone is already doing it... why would you assume it's true?"

The crowd is loud. It's never been the compass. It drifts. It reacts. It dominates.

The crowd is often confident. It is seldom correct.

Truth doesn't drift. It stands—especially when it's outnumbered.

The Ark had room. Plenty of it. But almost no one chose to enter (Genesis 6:17–18; 7:7).

That has never changed.

It will not start now.

CHAPTER TWENTY

The Superspreader

How This Actually Spreads

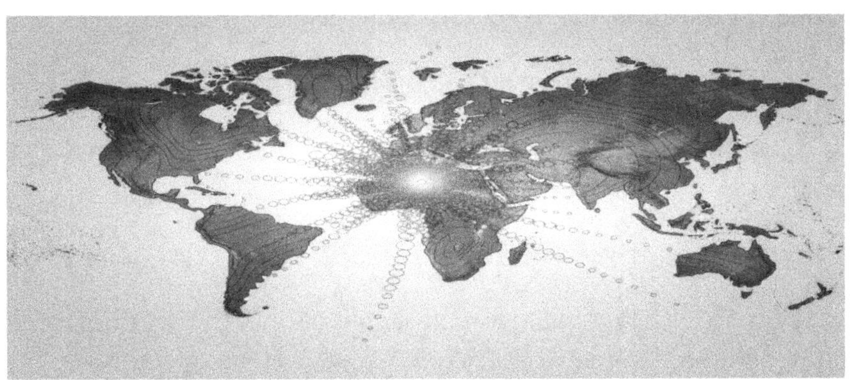

> *But you shall receive power when the Holy Spirit has come upon you; and you shall be witnesses to Me in Jerusalem, and in all Judea and Samaria, and to the end of the earth.*
>
> — Acts 1:8

Most viruses never become pandemics. They appear quietly. They infect a few people. Then they vanish. History's full of outbreaks that never left the room.

Movements behave the same way. Most burn hot for a moment and then fade into history.

Christianity did the opposite.

In just a few centuries, obscure fishermen from Galilee rattled the most powerful civilization on earth: the Roman Empire.

The mystery isn't *whether* it spread. It's *how*.

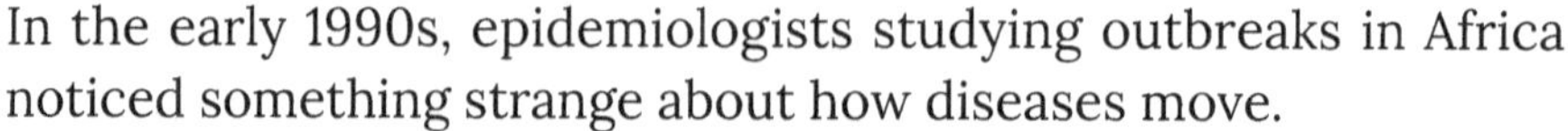

In the early 1990s, epidemiologists studying outbreaks in Africa noticed something strange about how diseases move.

Most infected people passed the disease to no one.

They became sick, recovered or died, and the virus stopped with them.

But occasionally the pattern changed.

One person with high exposure and high connectivity would infect ten people. Or twenty. Or fifty.

These rare individuals became known as *superspreaders*.[1]

Once you see that pattern, Acts stops looking like a theology textbook and starts looking like an epidemiology report.

The story starts small.

It began with 120 believers huddled in an upper room in Jerusalem (Acts 1:15).

And if you watch closely, you can spot the moment when the transmission rate spikes.

It wasn't when Jesus preached to crowds.

It was when fire fell on the carriers.

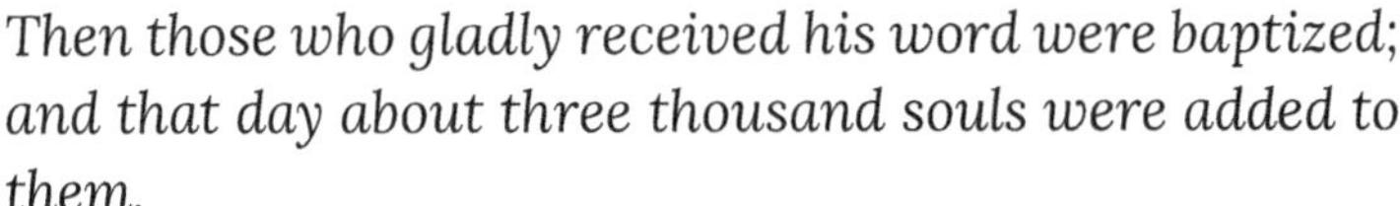

Then those who gladly received his word were baptized; and that day about three thousand souls were added to them.

— Acts 2:41

Before Pentecost, the disciples were effectively quarantined. They had the message. But they lacked the power, and perhaps the nerve, to spread it.

Then something changed.

Wind. Fire. Power.

The Spirit fell on the disciples, and suddenly the message burst out like a spark in dry grass (Acts 2:1–4).

Peter stood up and preached (Acts 2:14).

Jesus had given him the keys, not to build a throne, but to open a door (Matthew 16:19). And when the moment came, Peter unlocked it and swung it wide open.

Three thousand people were baptized in a single day. An outbreak had begun. It wouldn't stay contained.

The Ark had opened its doors.

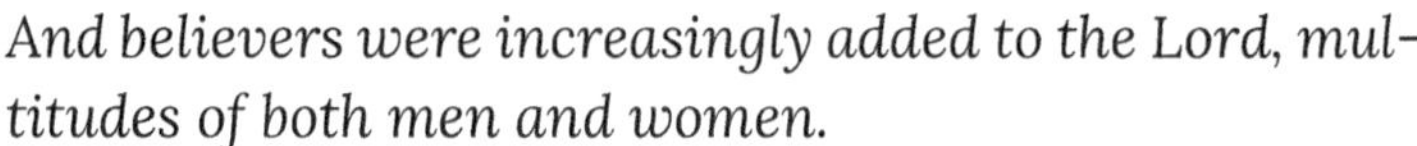

And believers were increasingly added to the Lord, multitudes of both men and women.

— Acts 5:14

Sociologist Rodney Stark spent decades studying why religions succeed or fail. By every rule in the book, this movement should have died immediately. It didn't—and the reason runs against intuition.

Movements that ask for *very little* tend to fall apart. Movements that ask for *everything* tend to grow.

Cheap religions become hobbies. People dabble, attend occasionally, drift in and out with little commitment.

But high-cost faiths create tight communities. They demand sacrifice, loyalty, and transformation.[2]

Early Christianity was brutally expensive. Converts could lose their jobs. They could lose their families. They could lose their lives.

And yet the movement spread because the apostles refused to soften the message.

Peter didn't say, "Follow your heart." He pointed to the water and said, "Repent, and let every one of you be baptized in the name of Jesus Christ for the remission of sins; and you shall receive the gift of the Holy Spirit" (Acts 2:38).

This became the movement's front door.

Public. Decisive. A line in the sand.

High cost. High commitment. High transmission.

> So they said, "Believe on the Lord Jesus Christ, and you
> will be saved, you and your household." Then they spoke
> the word of the Lord to him and to all who were in his
> house. And he took them the same hour of the night and
> washed their stripes. And immediately he and all his
> family were baptized.
>
> — Acts 16:31–33

But commitment alone doesn't explain the speed of transmission. How did the message travel so far so fast?

The answer lies in the structure of ancient society.

In the Roman world, the basic unit of life wasn't the individual. It was the *household*. Parents. Children. Servants. Workers. Cousins. Anyone connected to the household's daily life.

When the head of a household changed direction, the whole network moved with him. Acts shows this pattern over and over.

Cornelius gathered relatives and close friends to hear Peter. Lydia believed, and suddenly her entire household was standing in the water. The jailer in Philippi washed the prisoners' wounds. Before dawn, he and his whole family stepped into the water.

The Gospel moves through relationships the way electricity moves through wiring. Flip one switch, and the whole building lights up.

People rarely entered the Ark alone.

—◆◯◆—

> *Then Peter opened his mouth and said: "In truth I perceive that God shows no partiality. But in every nation whoever fears Him and works righteousness is accepted by Him."*
>
> — Acts 10:34–35

But the spread did something even more radical: it crossed lines.

First in Jerusalem. The disciples preached to Jews, and thousands responded.

Then Samaria. Philip preached to a people Jews had avoided for centuries. Samaritans were cultural outsiders—neither fully Jewish nor fully Gentile. The Gospel took root there too (Acts 8:5–12).

Then the final line was crossed. Peter walked into the house of a Roman centurion named Cornelius. A Gentile. A foreigner. An officer in the occupying army. The kind of person who represented the empire that executed Jesus.

Peter started speaking. And before he finished the sermon, the Spirit fell. Just like Pentecost.

Same power. Same fire. Different audience.

Right then, Peter realized something that changed everything. The Ark wasn't a Jewish vessel anymore.

It was a human one.

The Spirit opened the door. Peter still pointed them to the water (Acts 10:44–48).

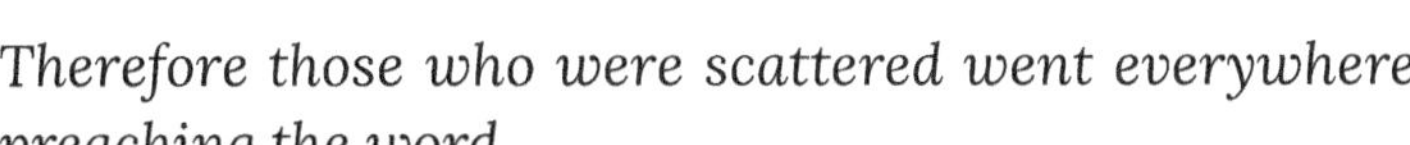

Therefore those who were scattered went everywhere preaching the word.

— Acts 8:4

And the outbreak continues. Not through celebrities. Through ordinary people.

Yes, Peter preached and Paul traveled.

But the real transmission happened through nameless believers—people whose stories never made the Bible. A merchant speaking to a customer. A servant whispering to a coworker. A neighbor speaking to a friend.

The Gospel has always spread this way.

Quietly.
Personally.
From one life to another.

You don't need a platform to be a carrier.

You just need to know where the water is.

These who have turned the world upside down have come here too.

— Acts 17:6

The early Christians didn't have the tools we associate with global influence. No printing press. No television. No social media.

Just conviction—and a message they refused to keep to themselves.

Within a few generations, the faith had reached every major city in the Roman Empire.

This outbreak refused to stay in the room. No one planned it. No one controlled it. It spread... because people carried it.

Two thousand years later, it still hasn't burned out. The storm keeps driving people toward the Ark whether they see it or not.

Because the strategy never changed.

God didn't build a crowd. He built carriers.

And carriers are not measured by what they received. They are measured by what they pass on.

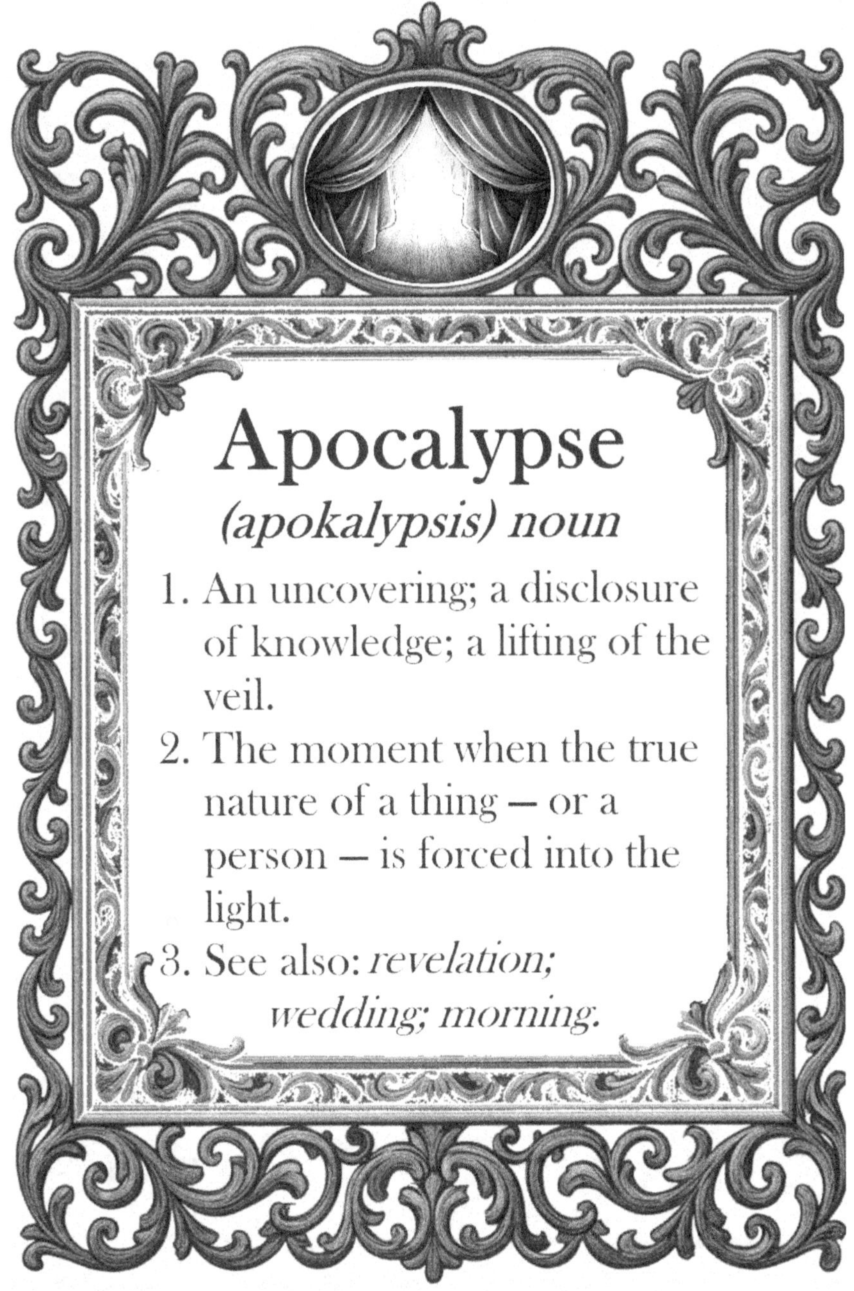

Apocalypse
(apokalypsis) noun
1. An uncovering; a disclosure of knowledge; a lifting of the veil.
2. The moment when the true nature of a thing — or a person — is forced into the light.
3. See also: revelation; wedding; morning.

CHAPTER TWENTY-ONE

The Normalcy Bias

Why Nothing Feels Urgent—Until It Is

> *But as the days of Noah were, so also will the coming of the Son of Man be.*
>
> — Matthew 24:37

I n AD 79, the people of Pompeii were living in a tomb. They just didn't realize the lid was about to close.

The warning signs weren't subtle.

Mount Vesuvius began to exhale smoke and ash. The ground shook. The air was thick with the scent of sulfur.

It was the geological equivalent of a scream: loud, violent, impossible to ignore.

And still, people stayed put. Not because they were stupid. Because they were... human.

They swept the ash off their porches. Opened their shops. Finished lunch.[1]

For most, it didn't feel like the end. When we're confronted with disaster, the mind reframes reality until it feels safe. It filters. It lies if it has to. It assumes that because the worst has never happened before, it never will.

Psychologists call this the *Normalcy Bias*.[2]

The volcano is just grumbling. The tremors will pass. One shake. One warning. One more reason to stay put.

Normal life becomes a sedative.

By the time the pyroclastic surge hit, many were still inside their homes. Some clutching jewelry. Others with bread in their hands.

The people of Pompeii weren't killed because they didn't see the signs.

They were killed because they explained them away.

For as in the days before the flood, they were eating and drinking, marrying and giving in marriage, until the day that Noah entered the ark, and did not know until the flood came and took them all away, so also will the coming of the Son of Man be.
— Matthew 24:38–39

Jesus said the end would look like that.

Not chaotic.
No panic. No sirens.
Busy.

That's the warning.

For 120 years, Noah built a massive Ark (Genesis 6:3; 1 Peter 3:20).

It wasn't hidden. It wasn't quiet. It stood right there in plain sight.

The hammering. The preaching (2 Peter 2:5).

At first, it was strange. Then familiar. Eventually ignored.

It became background noise.

Then the rain started.

The realization of judgment doesn't come with the first drop. It comes when the water reaches the door.

By then, the Ark is sealed (Genesis 7:16).

The Normalcy Bias comforts you right up until the moment it kills you.

Now when Jesus saw that he answered wisely, He said to him, "You are not far from the kingdom of God."
— Mark 12:34

"You are not far."

That sounds like good news until you remember Noah.

In Noah's day, many people were not far from the Ark. They lived nearby. They watched it being built. They heard the warnings.

They were close.

They still drowned (Genesis 7:21–23).

That is the cruelty of *almost*.

Almost obeyed. Almost entered. Almost safe.

Almost is close enough to comfort the conscience, but not close enough to survive the judgment. It gives you just enough religion to feel serious and just enough distance to remain unchanged.

Nobody outside the Ark had to hate Noah to drown. They didn't have to mock the pitch, curse the wood, or deny the clouds. They only had to stay where they were.

Near the door.
Near the warning.
Near the truth.

Outside.

To be "not far" is to live in the suburbs of salvation. You can see the skyline. You like the idea of it. Maybe you even visit on holidays.

But you don't live there.

Proximity, it turns out, is not a life-saving strategy.

Occupancy is.

Distance—no matter how small—still kills.

Knowing this first: that scoffers will come in the last days, walking according to their own lusts, and saying, "Where is the promise of His coming? For since the

fathers fell asleep, all things continue as they were from the beginning of creation."
— 2 Peter 3:3–4

Peter says the last days will sound like this.

"Relax. Nothing's changing."

Everything continues.

That belief feels stable.

It is deadly.

History isn't a loop. It's a countdown.

Creation began with a word (Genesis 1:3).

It will end with a trumpet (1 Corinthians 15:52; 1 Thessalonians 4:16).

For when they say, "Peace and safety!" then sudden destruction comes upon them, as labor pains upon a pregnant woman. And they shall not escape.
— 1 Thessalonians 5:3

We like those words.

Peace. Safety.

They feel solid and reliable. Completely normal.

We are living in the Pompeii of history.

Truth is bending (Isaiah 5:20).
Morality is softening.
Sin is treated as a lifestyle.

People sweep the ash off the porch.

Life goes on.

Kids to school.
Work keeps grinding.
Dinner at six.

Here's the lie:

Tomorrow will look like today.

Normal life will continue right up to the moment it doesn't.

The door has not yet shut (2 Corinthians 6:2).

For now.

But the sky is darkening.
The air is shifting.
The volcano isn't resting.

It's preparing.

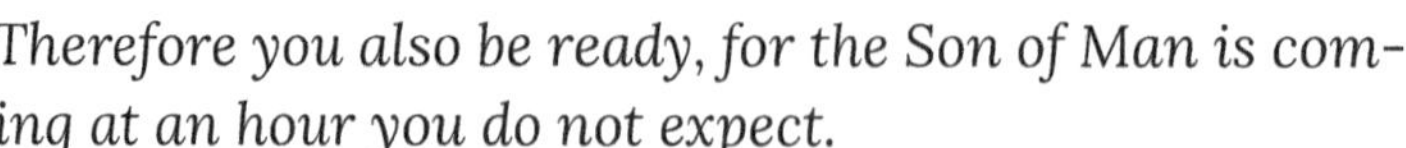

> *Therefore you also be ready, for the Son of Man is coming at an hour you do not expect.*
>
> — Matthew 24:44

Why don't people board the Ark?

Because nothing feels urgent.

Tomorrow looks dependable.
Everything feels… normal.

And normal is the most addictive drug on the planet.

It numbs you enough to ignore what matters most.

Catastrophe doesn't arrive without warning. It arrives after a series of ignored signals.

Until the moment when ignoring them isn't an option.

And by then—

the door is closed.

CHAPTER TWENTY-TWO

The Element Change

What Survives the Fire Doesn't Look the Same

> *But the day of the Lord will come as a thief in the night, in which the heavens will pass away with a great noise, and the elements will melt with fervent heat; both the earth and the works that are in it will be burned up.*
>
> — 2 Peter 3:10

A blacksmith doesn't test metal by looking at it. He puts it in the fire.

Paint bubbles. Impurities rise. Weak metal warps.

But gold?

Gold just sits there. It doesn't budge. It comes out cleaner than it was moments before.

Fire doesn't lie. It reveals what's there.

And according to Peter, the world is heading toward a test like that.

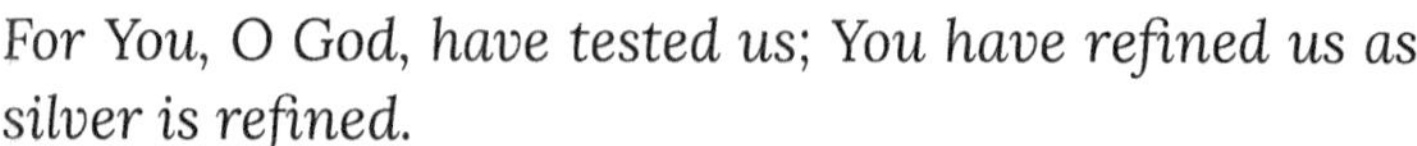

For You, O God, have tested us; You have refined us as silver is refined.

— Psalm 66:10

God doesn't repeat the same judgment. The Flood was a one-time weapon (Genesis 9:11).

But don't confuse restraint with indifference.

A promise not to drown the world isn't a promise to leave it alone.

It's a promise that judgment will not come that way again.

For this they willfully forget: that by the word of God the heavens were of old, and the earth standing out of water and in the water, by which the world that then existed perished, being flooded with water.

— 2 Peter 3:5–6

Peter paints a psychological profile of the skeptics in the last days.

"They willfully forget..."

This isn't ignorance. It's a choice. Suppression.

To admit that the world was judged once is to admit that God has the authority to judge it again.

That's uncomfortable. So we make the story more palatable—something we can accept without changing how we live.

The Flood becomes a myth, a metaphor, a bedtime story. Because if it's real, then we're not in control.

They aren't blind because they can't see.

They're blind because seeing would cost them too much.

But the heavens and the earth which are now preserved by the same word are reserved for fire until the day of judgment...

— 2 Peter 3:7

Peter says the world is preserved. But it isn't being preserved forever.

It's being preserved *for something.*

Fire.
Not water this time.
Fire.

Water and fire are opposites. Water drowns. Fire exposes.

One conceals what it takes. The other reveals what remains.

To survive water, you need something that floats. To survive fire, you need something that won't burn.

Wood floats beautifully.

But it burns.

If your spiritual strategy is built on effort, works, or moral reputation, you're not building a shelter. You're stacking kindling.

And if we're being honest, we are extremely good at falling in love with kindling.

The element has changed.

So the shelter must change too.

Each one's work will become clear; for the Day will declare it, because it will be revealed by fire; and the fire will test each one's work, of what sort it is.
— 1 Corinthians 3:13

Paul warned the early church that a day was coming when everything would be tested.

Fire doesn't care about appearances.

You can fake competence. You can fake conviction. You can even fake holiness if you know the language and stand in the right places at the right times.

Fire laughs at that. It tells the truth.

Paul describes the materials people build with: wood, hay, straw.

All gone in the blink of an eye.

But some things survive. Gold. Silver. Precious stones.

Fire doesn't destroy them. It refines them.

The church can't be built from materials that cannot last. Political power, cultural approval, and self-righteousness might float for a while.

They will not make it through the flames.

For our God is a consuming fire.

— Hebrews 12:29

Scripture describes God as a consuming fire. Not "God sends fire." God *is* a consuming fire.

Judgment isn't just punishment. It's exposure to His holiness.

Sin can't survive that presence. Nothing corrupt can stand in that light.

This is why the Resurrection matters so much.

On the Cross, Jesus stepped into the furnace and absorbed the full heat of judgment. And then He walked out the other side alive.

Not charred.
Not repaired.

Alive.

To be "in Christ" is to be clothed with the only righteousness that survives judgment (Galatians 3:27).

The fire is coming.

What matters is what you're wearing when it arrives.

⸺◆O◆⸺

Therefore, since all these things will be dissolved, what manner of persons ought you to be in holy conduct and godliness...

— 2 Peter 3:11

If you knew your house would burn tomorrow, would you spend today redecorating?

You wouldn't. You'd grab what matters and get out.

The coming fire isn't just a future headline. It rewrites the present. It changes our priorities. It changes our investments.

Because the only things that survive are the things that can stand the heat.

Everything else? Temporary. Flammable.

The world once drowned.

Next time it burns.

That is not imagery.

That is prophecy.

And when the fire comes, admiration will not matter. Respect will not matter. Proximity will not matter.

Only one thing will: whether you were found in Him.

CHAPTER TWENTY-THREE

The Blue Peter

The Signal You Can't Ignore Forever

> *So those that entered, male and female of all flesh, went in as God had commanded him; and the Lord shut him in.*
>
> — Genesis 7:16

In the age of sail, when a ship was preparing to leave harbor, the captain didn't chase his crew through taverns. He raised a flag—a blue rectangle with a white rectangle in the center.

The Blue Peter.

Everyone in the harbor knew what it meant.

We're leaving. Now.

And if you're still on shore when that flag goes up?

Congratulations. You live there now.

No debate. No extensions. No second call. Just a ship pulling away... and a harbor shrinking behind it.

Some men ran when they saw it. Dropped their drinks. Left conversations mid-sentence.

Others lingered. One more minute. One more story. One more excuse.

They watched the flag.

They didn't move.

> But be doers of the word, and not hearers only, deceiving yourselves.
>
> — James 1:22

In the days of Noah, no one was confused about the Ark. It stood there for years—visible, unavoidable, impossible to ignore, and easy to walk past.

People saw it. Heard the warnings. Watched the sky darken. They knew what Noah was building and why he was building it (Genesis 6:13–14).

But knowing is easy.

It doesn't move your feet.

It doesn't get you out of rising water.

Repent, and let every one of you be baptized in the name of Jesus Christ for the remission of sins; and you shall receive the gift of the Holy Spirit.

— Acts 2:38

Scripture describes salvation as a single motion.

Faith.
Repentance.
Baptism.

Movement.

Faith sees the Ark. The danger is real. The rescue isn't optional.

Repentance turns. It breaks agreement with the world behind you and points your life toward something else.

But neither of those steps gets you on board.

Baptism does.

The moment your feet leave the dock.

Remove any part, and nothing happens.

Faith without movement is agreement.
Repentance without entry is hesitation.
Baptism without faith is getting wet.

But when they come together, something irreversible happens.

You don't just understand the Ark.

You enter it (Romans 6:3–4).

He has delivered us from the power of darkness and conveyed us into the kingdom of the Son of His love.
— Colossians 1:13

No one boards a departing ship without leaving something behind.

The dock is familiar. Comfortable. Predictable.

It's where your routines live. Your relationships. Your identity.

And stepping onto the ship means you don't control where it goes.

That's why people hesitate.

Not because they don't understand. Because they do.

They know it costs something to leave.

So they stand close. Close enough to convince themselves they're already in. Close enough to build a life around something they haven't actually entered.

But close isn't inside. You can stand inches away and still be outside.

At some point, the rope drops.

And staying becomes a decision (Luke 9:62).

—◆◯◆—

Now as he reasoned about righteousness, self-control, and the judgment to come, Felix was afraid and answered, "Go away for now; when I have a convenient time I will call for you."

— Acts 24:25

People don't reject the truth as often as we think. They delay it.

"I will." "Soon." "Just not yet."

That's how people get left behind. Not because they didn't understand, but because they didn't move when movement was required.

The most dangerous word in the harbor isn't "no."

It's "later."

Later sounds responsible. Measured. In control.

It isn't.

Later is standing still with better language.

It has destroyed more people than rebellion ever did (Hebrews 10:26).

Rebellion is honest; it makes a choice.

Later is a liar. It pretends it hasn't.

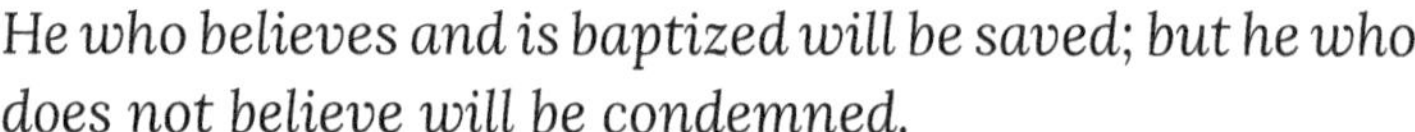

*He who believes and is baptized will be saved; but he who
does not believe will be condemned.*

— Mark 16:16

There is a line.

Not theoretical. Not symbolic. Real.

On one side: almost.
On the other: done.

Baptism is that line.

And like every line God draws, it is not only a command. It is a promise: "He who believes and is baptized will be saved" (Mark 16:16).

At Pentecost, Peter said the same thing another way: repent, be baptized, receive remission, receive the Spirit (Acts 2:38–39).

God is not handing the sinner another religious hoop to jump through. He is giving him a way out. Not as a symbol of something that already happened, but as the moment it happens.

It's when you stop negotiating and move. Not perfectly. Not with every question answered. But decisively.

Because the ship isn't waiting for your full clarity.

It's leaving.

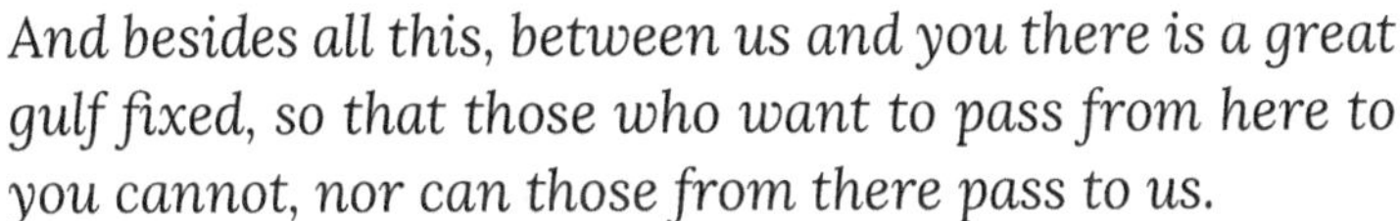

And besides all this, between us and you there is a great
gulf fixed, so that those who want to pass from here to
you cannot, nor can those from there pass to us.
                                        — Luke 16:26

There's always a moment when the distance becomes irreversible.

Not loud. Not dramatic. But measurable.

A few feet.
Then yards.
Then open water between you and the ship.

Suddenly the decision is no longer yours.

You're living with what you chose.

Or what you didn't.

The Blue Peter still flies. The signal has already been given.

Faith brings you to the dock. Repentance turns you toward the ship.

But baptism?

That's when you step onboard.

And once you leave, it's final. You don't belong to the dock any-more.

No halfway. No foot in both worlds.

You're either carried by the vessel or standing with everything that's about to go under.

The flag is up. The lines are cast off. The ship is moving.

The only question left isn't whether you understood.

It's whether you stayed.

Because staying was always a decision.

The Stink or the Storm?

Before the Door Closes

> *Behold, now is the accepted time; behold, now is the day of salvation.*
>
> — 2 Corinthians 6:2

We began this story in chaos.

Not in the garden of Eden, but in something raw and unformed.

Tohu vavohu.

Not peaceful or gentle. The kind of mess that doesn't stay contained.

Because chaos never does.

Left alone, it spreads. Then it settles in.

That's entropy.

The slow drift from order to disorder. From structure to breakdown. From "we're fine" to "how did this happen?"

Every system frays. Every empire cracks. Every life, eventually, wears out.

For most of human history, it has felt like entropy always wins.

The waters saw You, O God; the waters saw You, they were afraid; the depths also trembled.

— Psalm 77:16

The Bible calls that chaos something else. *Tehom.* The deep.

It swallows ships and erases borders. It doesn't answer to anyone.

Genesis opens with it (Genesis 1:2).
Noah's world drowns in it (Genesis 7:11–12).
The disciples—skilled fishermen—were terrified of it (Mark 4:37–41).
In Revelation, the Beast crawls out of it (Revelation 13:1).

The sea, in Scripture, is never just water.

It's instability.
Uncertainty.
A threat.

It's entropy made visible.

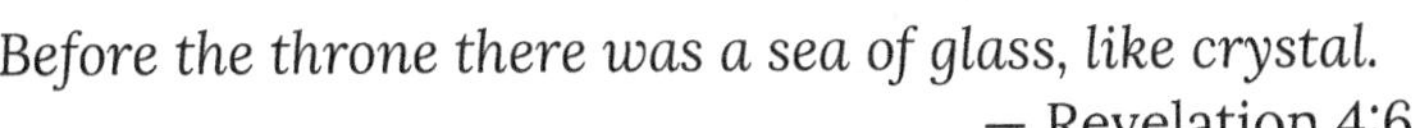

Before the throne there was a sea of glass, like crystal.
— Revelation 4:6

When John is pulled into the throne room of heaven, he sees something stunning.

A sea.

But it doesn't move (Revelation 4:6).

No waves. No roar. Just a flat, endless surface like polished glass.

God didn't remove the chaos.

He ruled it.

The thing that drowned the world now lies beneath His feet.

There is also an antitype which now saves us—baptism.
— 1 Peter 3:21

This is where the story's been heading all along.

In Genesis, the water threatens.
In the Flood, the water judges.
In baptism, the water becomes a grave.

But in Revelation, the water becomes a floor.

What once terrified now testifies.

The water wasn't the hero. It was the divide.

It swallowed the world—and lifted the Ark.

Same water.
Different outcome.

The chaos we met in the beginning doesn't get the final word.

Entropy had the first move. But it doesn't win the game.

There was a rainbow around the throne, in appearance like an emerald.

— Revelation 4:3

Around the throne hangs a bow.

Not drawn. Not aimed.

Hung.

Revelation describes it as emerald, circling the throne.

The same sign once set in the sky after the Flood.

Still unstrung. Still pointed away from the earth.

The message hasn't changed.

Judgment is certain.
Mercy is present.

Both are true at the same time.

For yet a little while, And He who is coming will come and will not tarry.

— Hebrews 10:37

We're not at the end of the story yet. We're in the middle.

The first Flood has already come. The next one has not.

This time, it won't be water.

The Ark is built.
The ramp is down.
The door is open.

But it won't stay open forever.

It never has.

And if I go and prepare a place for you, I will come again and receive you to Myself; that where I am, there you may be also.

— John 14:3

Jesus called Himself the Bridegroom.

In that world, weddings happened in two stages.

First, the covenant.

The price was paid.
The promise was sealed.

Then the groom left to prepare a place.

The bride waited. She did not know the day. But she knew the promise.

And she did not make herself beautiful. The Bridegroom did.

Then, suddenly, at the appointed time, he returned for his bride.

At night.
With a shout and a procession.

That's where we are right now.

The covenant has been made. The price is paid. The bride is being washed and made ready (Ephesians 5:25–27).

The Bridegroom will return (John 14:3; Matthew 25:6).

That's the moment we're waiting for.

Enter by the narrow gate ... Because narrow is the gate and difficult is the way which leads to life.
— Matthew 7:13–14

Let's be honest about the Ark. It was dark, uncomfortable, and it smelled.

There was plenty of shoveling. And no escape.

Outside, the world felt free. Open skies. Fresh air. Space to move—the broad path.

Until the rain came.

Then everything flipped.

The world outside became a prison.

The Ark—the thing everyone laughed at—became the only place left to survive.

The stink was temporary.

The storm was not.

And as it was in the days of Noah, so it will be also in the days of the Son of Man: They ate, they drank, they married wives, they were given in marriage, until the day that Noah entered the ark, and the flood came and destroyed them all.

— Luke 17:26–27

Here's the truth.

For those inside the Ark, this life is as bad as it gets. It only gets better.

For those outside the Ark, this life is as good as it gets. It only gets worse.

The door will close. The storm will come (Mark 13:33).

It isn't symbolic. It isn't theoretical.

It is final.

That is why the water still matters.

We are not baptized because we are saved.

We are baptized because we are lost.

Every argument will disappear.
Every delay will evaporate.
Every excuse will dissolve.

The sky is darkening. You can see it. You can feel it.

You can choose the stink. Or you can face the storm. You can't have both. And you won't escape both.

The choice has always been the same (Deuteronomy 30:19).

Where will you be?

Inside the Ark, or outside when the rain begins to fall?

Do you choose the stink... or the storm?

Before You Go

Y ou made it.

That already puts you in a smaller group than you might think. Most people don't finish things. Especially things that ask something of them.

So, thank you.

I'm going to ask you for one more favor.

Leave a review.

Did something stick?
Did something bother you?
Did you find yourself arguing with a page... and then losing?

Write that.

Not a thesis. Not a sermon. Just a few honest words.

That's how books travel.

Not marketing budgets. Not algorithms. Just people.

One reader leaves a few words, and somewhere else, someone hesitates a little less before opening the book.

And if you're not quite done thinking about all this—good. I'd love to hear from you.

Visit synesispress.com/#storm and click *Send Michael a Note*, or scan the QR code below.

Until then...

Keep your footing.
Watch the horizon.
And don't drift.

You don't get to choose if the water rises.

Only where you stand when it does.

—Michael

About Michael

Michael Brian O'Flaherty is a "retired" software developer and life-long student of Scripture. After years of troubleshooting systems that would not listen, he began writing about people who often do the same. *The Stink or the Storm* is his first book.

Endnotes

Preface

1. A nod to Paul Valéry, who famously noted that a work is never finished, only abandoned.

Introduction

1. Ark Encounter, https://arkencounter.com.

The Gathering Storm

1. "Tohu wa-bohu", *Wikipedia*, https://en.wikipedia.org/wiki/Tohu_wa-bohu.

2. J.D. Unwin, *Sex and Culture*, *Wikipedia*, https://en.wikipedia.org/wiki/Sex_and_Culture.

The Gopherwood Box

1. "All Saved from Titanic After Collision," *The Washington Times*, April 15, 1912.

2. Dodge, Washington. *Eyewitness Account of the Sinking of the Titanic*, 1912. The Gilder Lehrman Institute of American History. https://www.gilderlehrman.org/history-resources/spotlight-primary-source/eyewitness-account-sinking-titanic-1912.

3. "The Loss of the S.S. Titanic Quotes," Bookey, https://www.bookey.app/book/the-loss-of-the-s-s-titanic/quote.

4. John Clayton, in *The Source*, observes that the Ark's biblical dimensions (300 cubits long, 50 cubits wide, and 30 cubits high) create a 6:1 length-to-width ratio, similar to the proportions of many modern ocean-going barges. These vessels are designed for stability rather than speed, which fits the Ark's stated purpose: survival. Clayton notes that this is especially striking because many ancient seafaring cultures built narrower, more maneuverable ships for coastal travel. Whatever one concludes about the mechanics of the Flood, the Ark's proportions read less like a mythic boat and more like a purpose-built floating refuge. Clayton doesn't write from a young-earth perspective, and I'm not trying to settle that debate here. I find the observation compelling.

The Storm

1. "Pinus contorta," *Wikipedia*, https://en.wikipedia.org/wiki/Pinus_cont orta#Ecology.

The War Bow

1. William Shatner described his 2021 Blue Origin space flight as "grief" at the sight of Earth's fragility. "My Trip to Space Was Supposed to Be a Celebration; Instead, It Felt Like a Funeral," *Variety*, October 6, 2022, https://variety.com/2022/tv/news/william-shatner-space-bold ly-go-excerpt-1235395113. See also "Overview Effect," *Wikipedia*, https:/ /en.wikipedia.org/wiki/Overview_effect.

2. Ronald Hendel, "The Rainbow in Ancient Context," *TheTorah.com*, 2016, https://thetorah.com/article/the-rainbow-in-ancient-context

The Gyroscope

1. "New FAA Files Reveal Private Aircrafts Affected by U.S. Military's GPS Jamming During Tests," Engineering.com, February 1, 2021, https://www.engineering.com/new-faa-files-reveal-private-airc rafts-affected-by-u-s-militarys-gps-jamming-during-tests.

The Closed Source

1. Gregor Ojstersek, "How One Line of Code Caused a $60 Million Loss," The Engineer's Codex, https://read.engineerscodex.com/p/how-one-l ine-of-code-caused-a-60.

The Embassy

1. Hebrew University of Jerusalem, "First seal impression of an Israelite or Judean king ever exposed in situ in a scientific archaeological excavation," ScienceDaily, https://www.sciencedaily.com/releases/2015/12/151202 132519.htm.

The Fugazi

1. Allison Chase, "Fed's Counterfeiting Experts Fight Flow of Fake Money," Federal Reserve Bank of Boston, Massachu- setts, https://www.bostonfed.org/news-and-events/news/2019/10/c ounterfeiting-experts-at-boston-fed-fight-flow-of-fake-money.aspx .

2. "$160,000 in Jewelry Bought with Fake Money by 2 Men at Boston Jewelry Store, DA Says," CBS News Boston, August 14, 2025, https://www.cb- snews.com/boston/news/stolen-jewelry-boston-downtown-crossing.

3. "Tennessee Man Bought More Than $100,000 of Jewelry with Fake Money, DA Says," *YouTube* video, 0:32, posted by "CBS Boston," August 13, 2025, https://www.youtube.com/watch?v=DXt-aw8ATbA.

4. This section is a nod to my grandmother, Hazel O'Flaherty. She served on a counterfeiting jury. Her story inspired this chapter.

The Driftwood

1. London Fire Brigade Museum, "Early Insurance Brigades," London Fire Brigade, https://www.london-fire.gov.uk/museum/london-fire-brigad e-history-and-stories/early-insurance-brigades .

2. "Genericide," *Legal Information Institute*, Cornell Law School, https://w ww.law.cornell.edu/wex/genericide.

The Cosmic Mikvah

1. Aderin-Pocock, Maggie. *Webb's Universe: The Space Telescope Images That Reveal Our Cosmic History*. London: Michael O'Mara Books, 2024.

2. Mary Douglas, *Purity and Danger: An Analysis of Concepts of Pollution and Taboo* (London: Routledge & Kegan Paul, 1966), 35.

The Caisson

1. Frank Griggs Jr., "Brooklyn Bridge, Part 2," STRUCTURE magazine, November 2016, 51–54, https://www.structuremag.org/issues/2016-digital-is sues/november-2016.

2. Nostalgie de la boue (Émile Augier, 1855): Literally "nostalgia for the mud." The term implies more than just being stuck; it signifies a yearning for degradation. It describes the magnetic pull to return to the filth, even after one has been raised out of it. See also 2 Peter 2:22.

The Glass Floor

1. "Skywalk," Grand Canyon West, https://grandcanyonwest.com/things-t o-do/skywalk.

The Placebo

1. Herbert Benson and Richard Friedman, "Harnessing the Power of the Placebo Effect and Renaming It 'Remembered Wellness,'" *Annual Review of Medicine* 47 (1996): 193–99, https://pubmed.ncbi.nlm.nih.gov/8712773.

2. Batsell Barrett Baxter summarized the balance well in *The Family of God*: "Grace makes salvation possible; obedient faith makes salvation actual."

The Probate

1. "1995 Greater Pittsburgh bank robberies," *Wikipedia*, https://en.wikiped ia.org/wiki/1995_Greater_Pittsburgh_bank_robberies.

The Burial Plot

1. "Capitis deminutio," *Wikipedia*, https://en.wikipedia.org/wiki/Capitis_ deminutio.

2. "Ancient Roman Clothing," UNRV *Roman History*, https://www.unrv.co m/clothing.php.

The Glass Cage

1. Mark Nelson, "Biosphere 2: What Really Happened?," *Dartmouth Alumni Magazine*, May–June 2018, https://dartmouthalumnimagazine.com/art icles/biosphere-2-what-really-happened.

2. "Hyperetes", *Wikipedia*, https://en.wikipedia.org/wiki/Hyperetes.

3. Spychalla, Craig, "Encounter with Dahmer Changed Minister's Life," *The Christian Chronicle*, December 15, 2004, https://christianchronicle.org /encounter-with-dahmer-changed-ministers-life. See also Roy Ratcliff's book, *Dark Journey, Deep Grace: Jeffrey Dahmer's Story of Faith*.

The Ten Percent

1. "Minority Rules: Scientists Discover Tipping Point for the Spread of Ideas," *ScienceDaily*, https://www.sciencedaily.com/releases/2011/07/1107251 90044.htm.

The Superspreader

1. Malcolm Gladwell, "The Superspreader," in *Revenge of the Tipping Point: Overstories, Superspreaders, and the Rise of Social Engineering* (New York: Little, Brown and Company, 2024).

2. Rodney Stark, *The Rise of Christianity: How the Obscure, Marginal Jesus Movement Became the Dominant Religious Force in the Western World* (San Francisco: HarperSanFrancisco, 1997).

The Normalcy Bias

212

1. History.com Editors, "Pompeii," *History.com*, https://www.history.com/topics/ancient-history/pompeii.

2. "Normalcy bias," *Wikipedia*, https://en.wikipedia.org/wiki/Normalcy_bias.